THE BOTTOM LINE
OF
Happiness

Financial Strategies & Exit Planning for
the Big-Hearted Business Owner™

Matthew Pardieck

Editing, design, and distribution by Bublish, Inc.

ISBN: 978-1-647045-09-8 (eBook)
ISBN: 978-1-647045-10-4 (paperback)

Dedication

This book is dedicated to my late sister, Rachel Hazelwood. Being the youngest of four siblings, she was in many ways the best parts of all of us. A big-hearted business owner herself, she dedicated her life to her family (including her husband KC and young son James) and those she cared about. She was a consummate healer. She was also the first author in our family. You can find her wonderful book *Looking Into Heaven: Faith and Healing Through Brain Cancer* on major online retailers. We miss her, but she's undoubtedly a lead soloist for God's choir in heaven.

Contents

Prologue

I started writing *The Bottom Line of Happiness* in 2019, though I started shaping my thoughts about the book many years ago. When the COVID-19 pandemic of 2020 started, much of the book was already written, even as I watched dramatic changes to the world around us and worked hard to guide my clients through the chaos. Certainly, much about 2020 could have made someone pessimistic about the direction of society or even about faith in our shared humanity. And certainly, you would be a fool not to be concerned about many issues of justice, fairness, and the decisions of leaders. But I have also seen many people take wonderful actions through the pandemic: businesses pivoting not only survive but to help others, such as providing PPE to health care workers; donations increasing dramatically, especially for the benefit of those most affected; advisors spending extra time interpreting and helping navigate rules surrounding government pandemic relief programs, and the majority of people adjusting how they work and play to protect the ones they love. Every balance sheet has assets and liabilities—the pandemic amplified both, but I witnessed firsthand the positive net worth of humanity and the key role of the Big-Hearted Business Owner™ in it. I also witnessed many of the ideas in the book utilized to great effect, specifically by helping owners make better decisions in the face of rapid change, understanding new and evolving sources of liquidity, and supporting needed causes with tax efficiency.

As I finish this book at the end of 2021, I certainly anticipate continued changes in the markets and tax laws, some of which may make a few of these specific ideas or techniques obsolete. But I believe the processes here have a lasting benefit to business owners committed to taking care of themselves, their family, their employees, their community, and their causes. I apologize for referencing an overused parable, but I believe it has much relevance: An old man saw a young man on a beach that was filled with stranded starfish. He was throwing them back into the water. The old man asked, "Son, do you really think you can make a difference?" The young man responded, "It did to that one." I hope this book in some way can help you leverage your ability to make a difference.

Y.I.S.T.T.P. (Yours in service to the pack—a kind reference to thought leader Ben Hunt, Founder of Epsilon Theory)

Matt Pardieck

A modern glass cockpit, which still includes a basic compass!
(Photo courtesy of CRAFT Flight Training, KCHS)

Introduction

Approximately half of all Americans are employed by small businesses. These companies are led by people who have contributed their time and treasure—often at great personal and financial risk—to build economic value and create jobs. That's why, in my mind, small business owners are heroes. They are architects of the American dream.

Yet a large subset of this successful group is driven by more than the bottom line of profits and financial gain. These small business owners strive not only to grow prosperous companies but to make a difference in the lives of their families, employees, and communities. They donate their time, resources, and money to nonprofits and heartfelt causes. They wish to make the world a better place and leave behind a meaningful legacy. For them, the pursuit of happiness and fulfillment means the pursuit of purpose. It is equally important to their bottom line. I call these amazing people Big-Hearted Business Owners (BHBOs), and I wrote this book for them. The BHBO understands that giving and adding value can lead to higher overall wealth for both themselves and society. This abundance mentality, which endeavors to benefit both sides of every transaction and believes that entrepreneurial ingenuity can solve nearly any problem, is a hallmark of the BHBO. They understand that giving frequently results in receiving.

Economic textbooks commonly discuss the finite number of supplies as a constraint on growth and economic activity. The assumption is that when these supplies are used, nothing remains to create wealth. Yet small business owners create something out of nothing all the time. When at their innovative best, entrepreneurs frequently make use of materials or ideas not previously considered valuable. In so doing, they create wealth for themselves and society not previously considered possible. There are countless examples of advances made by entrepreneurs looking for better ways to do things: Few cared about rare earth metals like dysprosium before cell phones, and solar power has grown from a dream to an economically feasible alternative.

The abundance mentality applies not only to creative problem solving but also to dealings with other people. Time or money spent on family or other personally energizing causes like charities (or sometimes just R&R) can motivate, refresh, and refocus leadership. The combination of a benefits package and a healthy work-life balance for employees typically leads to greater productivity. Businesses and their owners actively involved in their communities frequently enjoy the benefits of good press and favorable customer attitudes. Finally, the tax code holds numerous opportunities to benefit charities, employees, and family members with minimal or even positive impact on a business owner's lifestyle. Doing good and doing well are not mutually exclusive.

What are the drivers for a BHBO? Throughout this book, I will reference these drivers as a business owner's personal "true north": the values, ethics, and causes most near and dear to their heart. Finding and following your personal true north is an important part of everyone's life journey. For those who wish to experience authentic human happiness and fulfillment, this is essential work. Your true north is your fixed point in a spinning world. It helps you stay on track, even during life's rough patches. Everyone's true north is different, guided by their unique values, ethics, passions, and deeply held beliefs. For some, it is faith that calls them. Loyalty and dedication to family, friends, and community are also often strong divers for many BHBOs. Others are drawn to do great things based on principles like integrity, compassion, charity, and more. Whatever your true north, it is uniquely yours, as specific to you as your personality. Thus, the BHBO can be a collection of people who may agree on little else besides the belief in abundance and ingenuity: They can be Republican (Bill Koch of Koch Industries—author of *Good Profit*), Democrat (Yvon Chouinard and Vincent Stanley of Patagonia—authors of *The Responsible Company*), a focused builder of great wealth only to donate/transfer later in life (Warren Buffett has pledged to give the majority of his fortune to charity before he dies—and has donated billions in 2020 alone), or maintaining generosity through every stage of the business cycle (look around your community and you will find many such examples). This book is not written to promote a specific version of true north; it is to help you use yours to align your business and personal goals with specific tools and ideas that have saved people millions.

If you don't yet know your true north, but you're on the path to becoming a BHBO, this book will still have immense value for you. *The Bottom Line of Happiness* is designed to help people like you successfully navigate toward your desired destination (goals) while avoiding missteps that could throw you off course, or worse yet, completely derail your journey. As a wealth manager for over twenty-five years, I have unfortunately met far too many well-intentioned business owners who come into my office for the first time thinking they are on the right path, only to learn that some vague regulation, hidden compliance issue, arcane tax rule, or poor decision made twenty years ago will now keep them from realizing their dreams. Those are rough conversations for me.

I've written *The Bottom Line of Happiness* to prevent such difficulties from happening whenever possible. The contents of this book offer a primer for BHBOs who are willing to make their true north a priority and use it as a guide for their plans. With the proper guidance,

BHBO cannot only arrive at their destination as guided by their true north, they can even accelerate their journey to that happy place.

Running and growing a successful business is immensely complicated, so I've taken the best of my practical tools for busy owners and included them in each chapter. They can help you avoid or overcome seen and unseen obstacles (taxes, liability, risk, and wasted time) and align your personal and business goals. Along the way, I'll ask and answer a lot of questions that will help you chart the best course to your destination:

- How do you incorporate your personal goals and values into the management of your business?
- How do you choose and manage personal and business advisors to help you make decisions that help your business and your goals?
- How does the type of business I operate affect the types of financing/access to capital available? the ways to build wealth for my family and those important to me? the tax savings tools available for my business as I grow? the best exit options for my business?
- What issues should I consider from a tax and management standpoint if I have a family business?
- What are tax-efficient ways to incorporate charitable giving consistent with my goals?
- How can I tell if a proposed exit will meet my goals? How can I minimize the tax?
- How do I manage a financial balance sheet after an exit and continue to live a life with purpose?

As your guide on this journey, let me tell you a bit about myself. In addition to being a seasoned wealth manager with four professional designations, I am also a trained aeronautical engineer and former flight instructor. As a result, many of my analogies about navigating to your destination are taken from my years in the cockpit. I hope you don't mind. My engineering brain also loves solving complicated problems, which comes in handy in the complex world of business.

Having worked in different industries and being a small business owner myself, I bring a broad skill set to my work. I have experience with sophisticated insurance-based tax strategies, investment banking focusing on employee stock ownership plans, the use of captive insurance companies to mitigate risk and build wealth for employees and family members, employee benefits consulting, various uses of charitable trusts, and the use of sophisticated financial modeling. I have helped clients through nearly every kind of exit, from family successions using estate planning techniques to purchases by private equity firms.

More importantly, I love what I do. I have had the unique pleasure of working with hundreds of small business owners from startup to exit. I love helping owners reach their destination while staying aligned with their true north—however they define it—after many years of hard work. Though each client is driven by a different set of values and beliefs, they all share a passion or a mission that drives them inexorably toward their goals. Having a front-row seat to their amazing work is deeply gratifying. If you are a BHBO, I'd be honored to show you how to navigate to *your* destination. Let's get started.

CHAPTER 1

A Compass to Your True North

"GO CONFIDENTLY IN THE DIRECTION OF YOUR DREAMS.
LIVE THE LIFE YOU IMAGINED."
–HENRY DAVID THOREAU

When flying, many of my passengers have marveled at not only the technology in the modern cockpit but also at the incongruity of the simple compass sitting amidst all the modern computerized instruments. Even with all these modern gadgets in a cockpit, every aircraft is still required to have this basic compass. It remains among the most timeless and reliable of all navigation instruments. It doesn't depend on man-made power to operate. It finds true north regardless of which direction the airplane is pointed. And it operates flawlessly as long as nothing blocks it from rotating freely.

Finding and following one's personal true north is an important part of everyone's journey through life. I believe it is an essential element in the pursuit of happiness and fulfillment. In this context, true north is defined as the values, ethics, and causes most near and dear to your heart, such as faith, work ethic, loyalty, dedication to family or others who are important to you, integrity, compassion, charity. These are the business owner's "why." These are the guiding set of values that define you as a big-hearted business owner (BHBO) and give you purpose. The ability to make money from a business is a fantastic gift, but your own true north will help you figure out how your business can also enhance meaning. Have you thought actively about your guiding principles? Many books are dedicated to helping people find their true north, and most BHBOs, wanting to help family, employees, charities, and community, are already far along in their journey toward identifying theirs. They may know in their core what is important to them. If you have not spent time identifying your own, I will share a process at the end of this chapter that will help you get started. But I bet you already know your "why" deep in your heart, even if it is not yet deliberately expressed.

I don't believe merely being conscious of your true north is enough. It can be easy to get distracted from your values and temporarily forget them in times of stress, especially during big decisions. Thus, it is equally important that you write down your values in the form of a mission statement. The mission statement then becomes your important compass for reference—the instrument in your cockpit helping you navigate your journey. When you are doing long-term planning, when you are meeting with your advisors, when you are deliberating over important decisions, your mission statement can help guide your way into making the decisions that are most aligned with your values. Throughout the book, I will mention compass and true north almost interchangeably since your mission statement is nothing more than a written reference of your true north.

But how do these core values help you navigate your business and personal decisions?

There is a saying in aviation: "There are old pilots and there are bold pilots, but there are no old, bold pilots." Pilots, like business owners, are accustomed to managing risk. Aviation, like entrepreneurship, is unforgiving yet incredibly rewarding. It is one of many reasons I believe aviation analogies fit well in the context of entrepreneurship. The professional pilot who makes it safely to their destination does not simply kick the tires, light the fires, and fly by the seat of their pants—as the old aviation saying goes. These pilots have considerable training, planning, and help from a good team. The same is true for those who wish to start, grow, and exit from successful businesses. This foundation is even more important for the BHBO because these owners do not simply want to land at a destination filled with riches—though that is certainly nice—they are also guided by their true north, which sometimes takes them on a slightly different path. The goals you have set for yourself through a written plan (discussed later in the book) become your destination. While financial independence may be a common and laudable goal for many, the BHBO uses their compass (mission statement) to make sure they reach the destination while remaining consistent with their values.

The process a business owner has of staying on course and reaching their goals is similar to that which a pilot follows planning and making a successful flight:

- A pilot must understand the type of plane they're flying, as it affects their mission and every aspect of flight, most especially their landing.
- While remaining in full control, the pilot in command must look for guidance from team members such as air traffic controllers and ground crew to make sure the plane remains reliable and doesn't fly into thunderstorms or other aircraft.
- They understand how to read their instruments to be sure systems are green and the aircraft remains under control and on course.
- The pilot understands emergency checklists and has prepared for any emergency.

- The pilot does what they can to make their passengers comfortable during flight as they work to keep the aircraft as efficient as possible.
- The pilot prepares for landing long before flare and knows how their aircraft will react.
- The pilot wants the landing to be smooth so that they and their passengers can enjoy the destination.
- Finally, and importantly, the pilot makes thousands of important decisions during the flight, referencing the compass, all to be sure they're headed in the right direction.

How can you use your compass and this book to reach your destination more efficiently? The path of the BHBO is not necessarily the easiest, but many tools exist to make the process more efficient while helping to avoid potential pitfalls. Following are a few examples. What if you could direct your tax dollars to charities, employees, or family members? While there certainly isn't a tax document that allows this option, many techniques exist within existing tax laws that allow business owners to do exactly that. Considering that most of your balance sheet is likely before taxes (the value of your business, the value of your 401k, the value of your real estate), the opportunity to take greater control over your full balance sheet is significant. As you know, if you write a big tax check to the IRS, nobody is going to send you a thank-you note. Put that same amount in a check to a charity and you can watch the immediate impact of your gift. You might even receive that thank-you note.

There are many ways a well-advised BHBO can more easily navigate toward favorable outcomes. However, I have used many of the strategies outlined in this book in my own practice, and they have saved my clients millions of dollars in taxes or hundreds of hours of time:

> **Charitable gift before business sale.** Properly structured, a charitable gift made *before* a business sale (letter of intent) can help you avoid capital gains taxes on the gifted assets.

Otherwise, taxes must still be paid, even if the gift is made immediately after the sale. For a $1 million gift, the result of making the gift before the sale saves at least $150,000. Of course, you must know how much you can afford to give prior to the sale. You must also know the likely sale price. These pieces of information are both integral parts of the planning process. It can even boost income for your family personally during retirement if combined with a charitable remainder trust—with charity ultimately receiving proceeds after you've passed away.

Cross-tested retirement plan. Properly structured, these plans can redirect corporate tax money to your employees *and* increase the amount you and your family can defer into a retirement plan. It is not uncommon to save or redirect more than $100,000 in taxes per year using this and other retirement-plan strategies.

Sale to an ESOP. While quite complicated, an ESOP can permanently defer capital gains taxes on a company's sale, provide tax deductions for both the principal and the interest of a financed sale, and leave the remaining company completely tax exempt. These tax benefits—which are redirected to your family and employees—can count into the millions of dollars.

Estate planning. The top rate of estate taxes in 2021 is up to 40 percent of the total value of your net balance sheet. Indeed, this means a $100 million estate would need to pay up to $40 million to the government within nine months. Imagine the devastation to unprepared businesses and families. Significant planning opportunities exist to dramatically reduce the tax burden, with the amount saved going to charities and/or family.

While opportunities abound for the savvy, well-advised BHBO, dangers lurk for the ill-informed. Just like pilots must navigate through or around strong winds, lightning, and bad weather, so must BHBO steer clear of visible and invisible threats to their business. This requires reliable instruments, a good group of air traffic controllers, and a good process because what you do not see can indeed hurt you. In my many years in the financial industry, I've seen surprises cause major trouble for small business owners. Here are just a few:

- A judgment against a business owner that results in balance sheet decimation
- Improperly administered retirement plans that leave owners personally liable
- Certain succession plans (like employee buyouts improperly structured) that result in taxes over 70 percent
- Improper gifting to family members, such as estate taxes being added to income or capital gains taxes, that results in taxes over 70 percent
- Minor children without a named guardian or trustee become wards of the state, their inherited assets frozen. This is horrifying for all involved, even if it's only temporary.
- After a death, a business or other illiquid assets (like real estate) can be forced to liquidate at a huge loss. Absent a succession plan, survivors may be forced to pay estate taxes within nine months of the death. Both the loss of goodwill and taxes can represent well over 50 percent of business value.
- A business owner, unable to loosen their grip on control, who finds themselves inescapably tied to their business as their succession/liquidation/selling options wither and business value disappears

Sorry if this sounds alarmist, but many BHBOs have suffered losses like these—and all could have been avoided with a good process. Yet, according to a 2017 Nationwide Insurance poll of more than a thousand small business owners, three out of five have no succession plan for their business—nothing. That's 60 percent! The reasons for this all too common oversight are complex:

- Forty-seven percent of business owners think succession planning isn't necessary.
- Thirty-three percent of business owners don't know when to create a succession plan. Breaking this down further, 11 percent aren't sure whom to work with in crafting a plan, and 11 percent simply don't feel they have the time to plan.
- Fourteen percent of business owners don't want to relinquish their life's work, so they ignore the fact that they need to plan.
- Eight percent of business owners feel overwhelmed by government regulations.

Is estate planning any better? Sadly, no: According to a 2020 report by caring.com and research firm YouGov, less than one-third of Americans have a will—including less than 50 percent of people over age 55. As baby boomers have just started reaching 65, Cerulli and Associates estimate the $68 trillion in assets will transfer in the next twenty-five years—the largest by far in history. The financial risk of this problem runs into the trillions of dollars. (In the next chapter, I will cover some of the traps that can obstruct planning by owners.)

Aligning Business and Personal Goals

As you can probably see by now, BHBOs plan and exit their businesses a little differently. While maximizing cash flow and business value are important to a BHBO, it's the ability to effectively leverage their business to reach destinations aligned with their values that really matters. Indeed, this connection between the personal true north of the BHBO and the direction of the business as aligned with an owner's true north and personal mission represents the magic and promise of the processes in this book. It requires strategic planning, effective use of sophisticated financial techniques, and expert guidance to avoid headwinds and ride tailwinds—all elements of a good process. Following are five key planning areas that will be discussed in greater detail in this book:

Minimize taxes. Taking greater control over the social assets within your business and personal balance sheet can have a tremendous financial impact on the people, causes, and missions consistent with your true north.

Reduce risk. Business owners face far more risk than their employees when it comes to a company's balance sheet. Corporate and personal liabilities, mortality and human frailty, regulatory penalties, market fluctuations, and casualty risks are all good areas to explore when it comes to reducing your risk as a BHBO.

Make informed financial decisions. When it comes to decisions about the financial assets and liabilities on your balance sheet, careful consideration from a variety of angles is required. With the help of your advisors, you must understand liquidity management, appropriate use of leverage, building and managing financial assets, and the selection of the best financial tools and strategies to grow wealth. The choices you make in this area can either derail your journey or accelerate the growth of your corporate and personal net worth.

Help your important people/causes. Using the most efficient tools to leverage your resources is a strong theme of this book. This includes the right tools for helping many situations: funding college education, employee benefits that enroll higher levels of engagement, assisting special needs children, making tax-smart gifts to charities, heirs, and others. However, helping the people or organizations you care about does not always involve monetary gifting. A good advisory team can help you evaluate other ways to empower your most important people and causes. Ethical wills—documents that share important wisdom, guidance, or leadership to beloved charities—as well as mentoring to new start-up entrepreneurs are two such examples.

Defining and leaving a legacy. How do you hope to be remembered? Legacy planning can be as simple as a heartfelt message and impeccable reputation, or it can be as sophisticated as creating numerous trusts and succession tools. The compass can again help you decide and implement the legacy that is right for you.

Finding Your True North and Writing Your Mission Statement

The compass should be your most reliable instrument—pointing to your true north, regardless of your current direction. If you have not yet written out your mission statement and identified your true north, this section can get you started. Certainly, I suspect most BHBOs are far along in this process as they are typically students of wisdom literature. Having also read many books and attended many seminars on the topic, I believe most have these three commonalities:

- You must set aside dedicated time away from all distractions.
- Take a few deep, slow breaths and clear your mind.
- In the manner you find most meaningful, get in touch with your core self. A great way to do this is by imagining your funeral or deathbed. Picture what you want people to say about you. Picture what you hoped you accomplished. Picture the people you most want to see. Picture the values that appear to you.
- Write them all down, do not judge yourself.

- After a break, take some time looking through your notes and circle the ones you believe are most representative of you.

Following are some thought-provoking questions I have found useful in helping clients articulate their true north:

• Who are the people most important to you?
• What are the values you hold most dear?
• What is the source of those values?
• How do you want to be remembered?
• What causes do you support passionately?
• What does success look like to you, monetary or nonmonetary?
• Where you are happiest? Describe it: Who is around you? What are you doing? What is your perfect day?

Congratulations, now you have a great written start on your true north!

Every business owner will encounter significant obstacles to success, many of which may seem insurmountable. Indeed, I am not aware of any client who didn't at some point wonder how they were going to make payroll. These obstacles include cash flow problems, losing a key client, losing a key employee, a bad economy, supply chain disruptions, lawsuits, new competitors—the list is endless. Even though business owners are generally a competitive bunch, and the financial rewards can be worth these risks, that is rarely enough motivation to overcome these setbacks. The BHBO almost always has something else: a higher purpose that helps motivate them through difficult times. Do you believe the items written in this first exercise can motivate you to overcome future obstacles? If so, you remain on the right track.

The next step is to convert your notes from the true north brainstorm into a workable personal mission statement. You can choose any format since your goal is to coalesce your true north into a few lines that feel right. For an idea on how these look for others, I've listed a few on my website, and you can certainly find many through an internet search. I will list some more extensive resources later, but for a good start see the following suggestions:

- Group your brainstorming answers into different categories, such as vision, values, and roles. You may have more in one category versus another; that is certainly okay.
- Rank them in order of importance within the categories. Do some trigger additional thoughts? Do some need to be reworded? Do they continue to ring true?
- Start writing sentences compiling these lists. Again, feel free to use any format. You might start with something simple that begins with "I am . . ." or "I believe . . ." or "I will . . ." It doesn't have to be complicated.

You could also hire professionals or purchase books and go through a more formal process of writing your mission statement. One of my favorites that I followed many years ago was the book *Seven Habits of Highly Effective People* by Steven Covey. This book, written in 1989, has inspired many other books and people on such areas as mission statements, principle-centered leadership (also the name of another Covey book), productivity, and motivation. His second chapter, "Beginning with the End in Mind," outlines in more detail a process I highlighted earlier in the chapter. Covey even has a website designed to help people write mission statements.

Another effective way to write a mission statement is with the help of a formal peer group, like Vistage, C12, The Alternative Board, your church, or other groups in your community. Regular meetings with other business owners can be a powerful tool not only to share common problems and solutions but also to help you find your true north. Most professionally organized groups bring in thought leaders and hold members accountable to goals that are consistent with their values.

Having watched many business owners grow and build wealth, I have seen this BHBO sometimes wrestle with the fear that money will somehow make them a bad person. Consider the verse from 1 Timothy 6:10 in the New Testament: "For the love of money is the root of all kinds of evil." Or from Lord Acton: "Power tends to corrupt; absolute power corrupts absolutely." Yet upon careful reading (and prayer), these passages state clearly that it is the *love* of money—not money itself—that is named as a source of evil. Money is a tool that can be used for noble and ignoble reasons. More important than the money are the personality and ethics of the bearer, as money magnifies this personality. If you were a good person while the poor owner of a startup, you are likely to remain a good person after building a large business. However, being mindful of your ideal self and referencing the compass of your mission statement can help keep you on course to being the person who makes you proud. It is the starting point for a rewarding journey.

As a financial and business advisor, I've watched hundreds of entrepreneurs reach their unique destinations despite differing paths and values. What connected them was their unique true north—guided by a passion or mission that drove them inexorably toward their goals. Having a front-row seat to their amazing work is one of the most gratifying parts of my job.

I know some of you may be impatient and want to fast forward to some of the techniques or exit strategies I promised that are included in this book, but I believe the establishment of these foundations are critically important to your ability to utilize these techniques effectively, just like the pilot who plans the flight before takeoff. Choosing your destination, or setting your goals, is the topic of the next chapter, along with the importance of starting early.

Chapter 2

Begin Early with the End in Mind

— — — — — — — — — —

"YOU MAY DELAY, BUT TIME WILL NOT."
—BENJAMIN FRANKLIN

Modern computing has streamlined flight planning exponentially, with many apps and tools that can calculate even international flights instantaneously. Even so, every pilot or ground crew still must determine the best route, the fuel requirements, the capabilities of the aircraft, and the impact of weather before they depart. As one pilot's adage goes: "It is better to be on the ground wishing you were in the air than in the air wishing you were on the ground!"

This planning begins as early as the mission requires. The more complex the mission, the earlier the planning starts. It took more than eight years for the most complex flight in history—Apollo 11's flight to the moon—to go from Kennedy's announcement to Armstrong's first lunar footsteps. Do you not consider your mission of critical importance and complexity?

As discussed in the previous chapter, most BHBOs started to identify their true north long ago—even if they may have not yet written down these values or figured out how that translates to more concrete plans. For most, a true north does not change over time—that's its beauty. However, BHBOs frequently forget their true north; it can get lost in everyday pressures and tasks. That's why writing out your mission statement—and referring to it often—is so important. How painful would it be to reach your destination and find that you'd landed at the wrong airport? Having your mission statement written out should be completed as early as possible, even if you're in the earliest stages of your business. Many a business owner has woken up to the distaste of a business morphed into an unrecognizable entity due to reactionary decisions made by an owner under stress.

Equally important yet much more common is the writing out of your goals—your journey's destination(s). Big-picture vision and goal setting are usually not a weakness for business owners. The challenge for the BHBO can be aligning your goals with your compass. Whereas every business owner needs to have financial goals set for their business and themselves, the BHBO will also incorporate their true north into nonfinancial goal setting. Consider the following questions:

- How will you define your legacy?
- What values do you hope to impart to family members?
- Where do you hope to improve your community?
- What does "taking care of employees" mean to you?

The answers to these questions also become part of your destination, along with financial security, business growth, and other business and financial goals. Just like the pilot, you must establish your destination and align your compass with your true north before taking off on your journey—even if you will undoubtedly have many course corrections along the way.

Almost by necessity, the entrepreneurial journey is littered with failure. There's the entrepreneur who lost his job, couldn't find another, and started a company without much thought. There's the entrepreneur who experienced multiple failures before finally finding a business formula that worked. There's the entrepreneur who was negatively impacted by regulatory changes or who simply started with too little cash. Many a business book has been written about the *importance* of early failure for entrepreneurs. It teaches the new business owner about true grit, perseverance, and toughness. As Dale Crighton, a real estate entrepreneur with many temporary failures, reminds us, failure or risk thereof isn't always bad: "When you're backed into a corner with seemingly no way out . . . it's the most creative you will ever be."

It's impossible to focus on long-term planning or an exit when you're struggling to meet payroll. However, incremental planning appropriate for the phase of your business should not be delayed. The earlier in your business cycle and the longer before you will need an exit, the simpler your plans and team need to be. This can be broken down into three stages of your business's life cycle:

> **Early:** At this stage, you should be thinking about how you'll incorporate your true north into how you treat employees, customers, and the community. You'll probably need a small team that consists of a CPA, attorney, banker, insurance agent, and financial advisor. Plans will focus on protecting cash and raising capital where possible to work toward business growth, including family members where appropriate, and developing a basic succession/estate plan.

> **Mid:** At this stage, a larger team more targeted for challenges unique to your business is needed, including consultants with skill sets appropriate to the size of the growing business; an initial exit strategy that leaves room for flexibility; planning more focused on protecting and increasing cash flows and minimizing taxes; and finding areas where the business can be leveraged to help achieve personal goals.

Late: At this stage, a team prepared to help with the type of exit you have planned is needed (such as investment bankers), including updates to estate plans such as legacy planning.

By now, a small percentage of you will have dropped everything you were doing and set aside a significant chunk of time to define your long-term goals and consider the next steps for an effective succession plan for yourself and your business. The majority, however, just went back to work.

How do I know this? Because many of us like to procrastinate, especially if it is something we may not fully understand and there isn't a triggering event that forces us to act—like writing your will before a long trip or after seeing a friend or family member devastated by a tragedy. But the stakes are so much higher for a multimillion-dollar business. Procrastination can hinder or even destroy a business owner's ability to navigate toward their destination, where they can fulfill their dreams. That's not good—and the point of this book is to help you avoid such traps.

Simple procrastination isn't the only way BHBOs lose their way. They face many distractions and traps—some external, others internal. Not having a process that uncovers your blind spots can unwittingly get you into trouble. In aviation, it is easy to fixate on one instrument and ignore others; it's one of the easiest ways to miss something important that can hurt you, like a thunderstorm. In chapter 6 I will discuss some ways to avoid some specific thunderstorms—traps for the unwary business owner—but here are a few examples:

- Minors cannot receive or use financial assets without a guardian or trustee. Thus, assets bequeathed to them without provisions to access the funds for their benefit could tie up the assets for months or even years. The naming of a guardian to care for minor children completely avoids this problem.
- With the death of a company founder who has no clear successor or organized plan for liquidation, many a business will

undergo a forced liquidation, taking away any goodwill or going-concern premiums the family would have otherwise enjoyed after the founder's death. This significantly reduces the value remaining for loved ones. I have even seen a widow without any business experience or knowledge of the business's industry attempt to maintain the business to preserve the deceased's legacy. She ended up losing several hundred thousand more, and the business was still ultimately closed. Happily, she still has most of her life insurance proceeds.

- Similarly, if a business has several owners and one of the business partners passes away, absent a plan, the surviving widow(er) inherits the business ownership. This creates many problems as the widow(er) and surviving partners typically argue over profits: The widower wants cash distributions, and owners want to invest in the business.

- While current estate tax laws apply to far fewer households than before, for estates in 2021, over $23.4 million is subject to federal tax rates of up to 40 percent, which can easily force liquidation of other assets just to pay the tax. While this may apply only to some estates, it still means millions of taxes are due on larger business holdings, all within nine months of an owner's death (this is the deadline for an estate tax return). Many planning tools exist to reduce or even eliminate this tax, especially for those with charitable intent—we will highlight many later in the book. For many business owners, the difference between planning and chance is many millions of dollars.

- Losing a lawsuit can destroy your balance sheet, especially if you have been careless with how you own, manage, and title your assets. Of course, conducting your business in a fair manner is always a good idea and helps reduce the likelihood of a lawsuit. However, a key factor affecting the likelihood of a lawsuit isn't necessarily whether you're careful or brazen; it's whether you have deep pockets. Bear in mind that plaintiff attorneys usually act on contingency, meaning they won't take a case unless they expect a payout. The deeper the pockets, the more interested they're likely to be in the case. Recent litigation has also expanded to new areas as attorneys gain experience and case law: retirement plan litigation. Structuring your holdings with asset protection in mind and carrying adequate liability coverage can reduce this risk.

- Becoming disabled can freeze personal and business assets without a written plan that assigns power of attorney. Imagine the impact on customers and suppliers when a business is unable to enter agreements, pay bills when an owner's oversight is required, or otherwise conduct normal business operations controlled by the disabled founder.

Unfortunately, there are many ways business owners can either blindly fly into these storms or botch an exit with a hard landing.

Flying Blind 1: "My Business Is Successful, So I'll Be Fine."

It's fun to win in the game of business, no doubt about it. But some prosperous business owners think their financial success will help them power through anything, so they focus exclusively on the business to the detriment of plans surrounding it. This is another example of fixating on one instrument at the expense of the rest. A pilot gets ensconced playing with a cool new GPS; meanwhile, the oil pressure reading is well into the red. Many events can decimate even the most successful business: lawsuits, health problems of family or key employees, or running afoul of government and regulatory entities, just to name a few. Consider that the US tax code is more than 6,500 pages long, and ERISA laws governing employee benefit plans take up around 500 pages.

You know your business like the back of your hand but being deliberate about scanning for other things that can hurt your business, maintaining an overall process, and having an experienced team of air traffic controllers can help you avoid this trap.

Flying Blind 2: "It Can't Happen to Me!"

Business owners are generally an optimistic bunch. Otherwise, why would anyone ever start a business with the knowledge that only approximately one in ten will succeed? Yet this optimism can make it easy to ignore the worst-case scenarios that could befall you or your business. Examples of things gone wrong abound in probate courts (which handle estates) in addition to stories I've seen in which an owner becomes disabled without a plan. It's still shocking to me how many brilliant, famous people have passed away without a will or estate plan—among them Abraham Lincoln, Joe Robbie (more later), and Howard Hughes. While Lincoln's estate was rather modest, Hughes's vast empire of real estate and businesses took the probate courts thirty-four years to reach closure. While this is an extreme example of a complicated and disorganized estate, lack of planning for our fragility does commonly create fiscal disasters. As they say, plan for the worst, hope for the best.

Flying Blind 3: Holes in Your Radar

Even in the modern air traffic system, there are some rare areas within the United States without radar coverage. In these areas, a pilot needs to use their onboard radar or their eyesight to stay away from thunderstorms or other aircraft. In the business world, it is important that your team of advisors has the experience and knowledge commensurate with the size and stage of your business or you could have similar gaps in radar coverage.

I sometimes hear, "it's all squared away." Joe Robbie, once owner of the Miami Dolphins and a prominent trial lawyer, passed away unexpectedly in 1990 at age 73 with a basic estate plan in place. Unfortunately, the estate plan was far too simple for his large estate and made no plans for the $43 million tax. The Dolphins were sold for $109 million in a forced liquidation. Worse than the tax, the liquidation forced the estate to sell the team for (likely) well below market value, as the franchise sold again 15 years later for a cool $1 billion. Had Robbie known what was to happen, would he have said everything was all "squared away"?

Sometimes a hard landing is unavoidable, such as a wind gust at the last moment before a touchdown. But many times, a hard landing happens because of poor preparation in the approach, especially for smaller airplanes. Following are ways a business owner can mess up their exit.

Hard Landing 1: "I Am the Business!"

The most common consequence of delay I see business owners fall into is making themselves essential to every aspect of the business they have created. They are in charge of sales, strategic direction, purchasing, marketing, human resources—the list goes on and on. Sure, it feels great to be needed. But as both the company and the owner get older, the institutional knowledge necessary to run the business becomes too concentrated in the owner's brain. Even worse, as the owner's net worth becomes more closely tied to the business, they tend to trust fewer people. I have seen many 70-year-old owners who feel trapped because they've created a business that can't survive without them.

Over time, this concentration of power and knowledge increases stress on the owner and discourages prospective buyers, who avoid businesses that are run this way. Buyers are typically looking for some combination of two core characteristics: a reliable or growing income stream and a business asset they can't replicate (such as proprietary business processes). Note that both characteristics depend on the purchaser being able to gain something completely independent of the owner. If these do not carry on with the business without the owner, buyers are not willing to pay nearly as much.

If a business owner never lets go of the reins and delegates knowledge and authority to others, as they get older, they'll have fewer and fewer options for an exit—and ever-decreasing business valuations. Ironically, the owner takes increasing amounts of control to protect their most valuable asset even as doing so craters its value. Ultimately, the business is sold for a fraction of its earlier value as the owner has limited selling options late past retirement.

Hard Landing 2: Arriving at the Wrong Airport

Every type of exit has merit, whether it's a buy/sell agreement, private equity buyout, ESOP, or others as discussed later in the book. Following are ways choosing either the wrong exit for *you* or not properly vetting your exit can result in a hard landing.

- **Selling to a private equity firm.** This option can be a spectacular exit for many, but perils abound for the unwary. Anne spent months personally researching private equity (PE) firms that might be interested in buying her profitable and growing business, figuring that was the best alternative since the local press had covered several local exits with compelling values. As she conducted the search by herself, she focused primarily on expected high valuations, local proximity, and experience in her industry. She chose one and began discussions focused primarily on negotiating a price—by herself. Without needing to compete through an auction process (competitive bidding for a company), the ultimate agreement had a high valuation, but a considerable portion of the sale was tied up in the future sale of "Newco" (a common term for a new entity created to purchase a business). The intent was for Newco to acquire, grow, and enjoy a second exit with an even higher valuation. The deal was consummated, and Anne received a very nice payout. Within a year, the firm let many of her key employees go. After two years, the strategic direction changed in a way that Anne found disagreeable. In the third year, Anne received a six-figure tax bill on "phantom income" as the PE firm reported significant earnings without making a distribution to pay the tax. None of the actions by the new ownership had been negotiated. Now, she's still waiting for the promised sale of her remaining equity position in the company, which may never happen. The exit was neither consistent with her true north, nor did it have the benefit of a team to vet the agreement.

- **Buy-sell agreement funded with life insurance.** Because it affords many tax benefits for both cash values and death benefits, life insurance can be a tremendous planning tool. As a mechanism for a living buyout to fund retirement, however, it has significant weaknesses if not structured properly. Harvey had a group of key people he believed could manage the business after his departure, wanted to take care of his family if something were to happen to him, and wanted a reasonable purchase price from his key employee purchasers when he retired. He had a friend in the insurance business who, along with an attorney, helped Harvey establish a good plan that would work wonderfully in the event of his passing. His team had dialed up his policies for death benefits—thus hurting cash value growth. Unfortunately, the cash values within the life insurance policies did not accumulate anywhere near the values needed for the employees to purchase the business. Ten years passed, and Harvey was forced to consider a completely different exit plan that would help fund retirement. Harvey's original exit plan could have used a better funding vehicle that took into consideration his complete vision.

Hard Landing 3: Where Did All the Money Go?

Eventually, as a business matures and the owner transitions from bootstrap to free cash flow, they will start to make some decisions about the use of these funds. Allocation of free cash flow toward investments that help foster business growth is an important and natural progression of business success. But what about the use of free cash flow toward personal goals to diversify your balance sheet and shelter you and your family from difficult business environments? This is especially important to service-oriented businesses, due to their more limited exit valuations.

- Charlie owned a small medical practice earning a competitive income and delighted in healing his patients. Doing what he loved and perfecting his medical craft for the benefit of his patients was both financially and emotionally rewarding. While living a comfortable lifestyle, Charlie had never considered the likely exit price he would receive for his practice—small medical practices usually sell for up to a modest one year's annual revenue—and didn't focus on building wealth outside of the practice. As he approached retirement, he discovered, upon further analysis of his company's retirement program, that it could have been structured to maximize contributions for himself if he had contributed more into his employees' accounts. The lost opportunity for tax savings reached over $1 million, and the lost opportunity to redirect tax dollars into his valued employees cost him nearly as much. He was forced to work much longer than anticipated to build a sufficient nest egg for his family.

Ideas without execution and preparation are merely pipe dreams. A financial plan incorporating your business, aligned with your true north, and guided by a good team of advisors is the flight plan needed to be sure you reach your intended destination. Assuming you have identified your true north and have written out your compass, the important next steps are envisioning your destination. This is probably every business owner's favorite task: goal setting! The difference here is the intentionality of linking business and personal goals with your compass top of mind:

1. Define your personal goals. Write out where you see yourself in three, five, and ten years. Consider the checklist from the previous chapter as a basis for these goals.
2. Think about the people and causes most important to you. How do you want to help them over these time frames?
3. Compare your personal goals to the goals for your business's growth. Are they consistent? Will one motivate the other?
4. If something unfortunate happens to you, what do you want for your family? For your business? For those people and causes important to you?
5. Tell important people in your life about personal goals as well as business goals—family, select friends, peer groups. Enroll their help in creating ways to hold yourself accountable to your goals.
6. It's lonely at the top—so consider joining or creating your group of CEO peers to share goals, hold each other accountable, and discuss common challenges.
7. Force yourself to step away from the business for increasingly extended periods to see how autonomous your business can be. Time away from the business can refresh your motivation and let you know if the business can operate without you, a key characteristic of a marketable business.

Lao-tzu, the sixth-century BC Chinese philosopher, is attributed as writing, "A journey of a thousand miles begins beneath one's feet." Your plans do not need to be perfect, but they do need to be congruent with "the ground beneath your feet," and you do need to take the first steps. Believe it or not, an airplane is off course 90 percent of the time, yet, by making hundreds of small course corrections based on its compass, it still reaches its destination. Set your personal goals, pick your team, and start your journey as soon as possible. And enjoy every one of your course corrections. In the next chapter, we will discuss the team, your air traffic controllers, helping you on the journey.

Chapter 3

Building Your Team

"GREAT THINGS IN BUSINESS ARE NEVER DONE BY ONE PERSON; THEY'RE DONE BY A TEAM OF PEOPLE."
–STEVE JOBS

Entrepreneurs are a fiercely independent bunch. They build things. They grow companies. They solve problems and overcome obstacles. In the beginning, most small business owners do all these things themselves. They don't yet have the financial resources to hire people. But then their companies grow, and they build a team of employees to grow with them. Without this team, the company would not be able to deliver the goods or services driving its success through growth. Still, that solo beginning and independent mindset shapes many business owners' decisions and actions throughout their companies' life spans.

Pilots are also an independent-thinking bunch. The Federal Aviation regulations give pilots ultimate responsibility and final decision making to the pilot in command. That person can even ignore the directions of air traffic controllers if they believe it's safest for the aircraft. Of course, they will have to answer for these decisions once on the ground. Similarly, the owner of a business maintains decision-making authority and faces full responsibility for their decisions.

When it comes to planning for your destination, you also need a team. The experts you gather around to serve as your compass help you steer clear of headwinds and storms while learning how to ride favorable tailwinds. They help get you fly efficiently and land the aircraft safely at your intended destination.

A BHBO's team brings expert knowledge of their unique specialties around many areas directly impacting you and your business. The type of expertise you need depends on where you are in your business growth, what type of business you run, and what your goals are. You'll need different advice and advisors if you're trying to take your company public than you will if you want to pass your company on to family members or employees. The former would require an investment banking team and perhaps more specialized attorneys, while the latter would need a CPA valuation expert, an estate attorney, and perhaps an ESOP specialist. The same goes for your line of business. If you're in services like I am, you need specialized CPAs, attorneys, bankers, and insurance people on your team. On the other hand, if you're a commercial contractor, you need people with similar titles but different areas of expertise because the laws, tax codes, and threats that impact your business are different from those of someone who runs a business in the service sector. But in general, your team will include experts in areas such as corporate structures, taxes, law, strategic planning, and finance.

A diverse team of experts can also offer you different perspectives from which to view your business, potentially uncovering opportunities you may not have thought of on your own. Without a diversity of ideas, you're likely to get cookie-cutter solutions. In addition, having a team brings balance to your decisions so that a decision in one area or made by one expert is less likely to negatively affect another critical area. Countless conditions exist where a good tax decision negatively affects asset protection; a good financial planning decision negatively affects banking; a good asset-protection decision negatively affects bonding or insurance. For instance, while it may make sense to distribute cash from the business to reduce potential liability, it may not leave enough money on the books to satisfy banking or bonding. Having a team that communicates well is critical to finding the middle ground that's best for you and your business.

Finally, the members of your advisory team act as trusted experts and guides, not simply specialists who can handle compliance requirements. They can also share their life wisdom, which can be helpful when the going gets tough. An experienced team is likely to have seen your issues before and have elegant solutions. It is also common for the team to know about potential business opportunities in your community and to make introductions to key people or knowledge. A good team connects you and your business to a legacy that you will both benefit from and pass on to those who follow in your footsteps.

I believe you should take the time to build a team with the same diligence and care you would choose a doctor if you needed critical treatment. While the outcomes of choosing a bad advisory team are certainly not as catastrophic as those of choosing a bad doctor, your potential gains from choosing carefully and strategically are limitless. No matter what a team member's skill set, there are certain important qualities that all team members should have:

- **Character.** This is a broad category subject to some interpretation, but in my opinion, this means the advisor is honest, treats you as they would themselves, and follows through on their promises. As a BHBO, you may have your own definition; follow that.
- **Professional excellence**. Many advisors have professional designations that can demonstrate a basic level of competence in their respective fields. However, excellence is shown in a desire to be at the top of their game—someone who learns constantly, seeks new ideas, does not assume they know

everything, and sees room for improvement in every aspect of their practice.

- **Experience.** While a bright upstart who is an avid reader/learner can certainly learn from others' experiences, I reflect on how my advice through the years has improved with time. Experience not only allows advisors to recognize many more potential problems and opportunities but also increases the likelihood that an advisor can offer new insights specific to you that aren't written in textbooks.

- **Proactive thinking.** Good pilots are told to always "stay ahead of the airplane," meaning to be prepared for the next step in their flight. Similarly, a good advisor is always a step ahead—as concerned with what will happen after the immediate next step as they are with what is happening now or what has already happened.

- **The right amount of rapport.** Having a good gut feeling about an advisor is important. However, don't confuse that gut intuition with feeling good because they tell you what you want to hear. They have to be willing to say what you *need* to hear—and you have to be willing to take it in. In an episode of his podcast *Revisionist History* titled "Pull the Goalie," Malcolm Gladwell discusses the difference between people who make decisions based on how others perceive them versus those who decide based on what they believe is objectively right—and placing them on a spectrum from golden retriever (agreeable and wants nothing more than to please its owner) to *Star Trek*'s Spock (disagreeable—in other words, doesn't care what you think). You do not want to hire a jerk who dispenses advice with no empathy but make sure your advisors can speak to you candidly.

While choosing friends and people who connect to your social circle can be a good way to filter advisors for character and rapport, be sure that excellence, experience, and proactivity are also present within your advisory team, especially as your business grows and decision making carries greater stakes. Next, we'll explore the different types of experts you should consider when you are building your team and how to manage them effectively so they can work as a cohesive group.

Whom Do You Need on Your Team?

There are many different areas of specialization that might be needed to create an effective advisory team to guide you to your destination. If you have a clear vision as to where you are going, then you are probably ready to bring together the team that can get you there. However, if you're still not sure of your ultimate destination, you might need to do some foundational work before you build your advisory team. Typically, one trusted advisor, such as a coach or professional mentor, can help you do this work before you build your team. After that, consider inviting some of these types of advisors to join your team, based on your goals and type of business:

Attorneys

Attorneys are an essential part of most advisory teams. They play many roles in helping guide businesses safely through diverse areas such as taxes, contracts, and regulation. It's important to hire an attorney with expertise relevant to your goals and where you are in your business. You wouldn't hire an orthopedic surgeon to perform open-heart surgery, right? The same sort of selection process is warranted with attorneys. Specializations for attorneys come primarily from experience, though attorneys sometimes will earn the rigorous Master of Laws (LLM) degree to better assist their clients within an area of specialization, such as tax, cyber, insurance, trade, government, or securities. Larger law firms split their specialties into different practice areas led by those with the most experience in them.

Attorneys enjoy a special right over and above all other advisors: attorney-client privilege. This means not even courts can compel an attorney to share information you have shared with them in private. This is quite important in sensitive areas that can be litigated so that you can speak freely with your attorney without fear that what you share can be released to an opposing party. With this privilege, they are also held to very high fiduciary standards and must represent only one party in any transaction. This means that they are required to advocate for that client in all business matters. Frequently this is why attorneys must conduct a conflict check before taking on a new client. They must make sure they do not represent two sides in a transaction.

Attorneys typically work on a retainer basis measured against an hourly rate. They may also have specific rate sheets for fees around documents and certain services. Some law firms will charge a subscription-based fee intended to cover most of the work required by small businesses. Attorneys are frequently the implementers on a team—they write the documents, represent you in legal actions, and are the final authority on interpreting legal issues.

Accountants

Like attorneys, accountants are also an essential part of any business owner's advisory team. Certified public accountants (CPAs) provide the record-keeping and advice necessary to prepare and file taxes for your personal and corporate returns. They also provide valuations for important assets, including businesses and properties, as well as the auditing services that are required by various regulatory agencies. They keep financial statements current and accurate and give you and those important to you a complete picture of your business's financial health when important decisions need to be made. A good CPA can help translate financial records into actionable ideas for business owners to help manage the business and minimize taxes.

Much like attorneys, there are many areas of specialization for CPAs, some of which don't have added designations. The CPA designation itself implies that accountants are competent generalists across all areas of specialization. Not surprisingly, this makes it equally important to review your CPA's experience in your businesses sector. For instance, I've seen CPAs focusing on health care help medical practices implement systems that track and streamline complicated medical billings that pay for their services many times over. I've seen contractor CPAs document and explain financial statements to bonding agents, resulting in the ability to bid on larger contracts. And of course, a good CPA will help you find nuggets in federal, state, and local tax codes that you likely would otherwise overlook, resulting in real money to accelerate your journey to your destination.

CPAs are regulated primarily by the American Institute of CPAs (AICPA) and the National Association of State Boards of Accountancy (NASBA), which administer the CPA exam; provide education; and enforce the profession's code of ethics, continuing education requirements, and disciplinary actions—all public information on the AICPA website. Unlike attorneys, CPAs can practice in any state. The profession does have several difficult designations reserved for the accounting profession; among them are the following:

- **CVA®:** A certified valuation analyst is a designation covering the valuation of many assets, most especially businesses. This designation holds tremendous weight by the IRS and is frequently required by parties in business in business transactions.

- **PFS®:** A personal financial specialist is a designation covering a broad area of financial planning topics issued to accountants by the AICPA. It is similar in scope to the CFP® (CERTIFIED FINANCIAL PLANNER™) designation discussed for financial advisors.

CPAs have two distinct compensation and engagement regimes: attest and non-attest. Attest means the CPA is required to avoid conflicts of interest, much like practicing attorneys, as they attest to reports such as audits, financial statements, fairness opinions, and valuations. The non-attest compensation model allows the CPA to be more flexible in compensation but forbids them to "attest" to the reports previously mentioned. If properly disclosed, this can allow commissions on products or services, assets under management, or other consulting arrangements.

On an advisory team, CPAs are frequently both the recorders and the navigators of the tax code. They provide the necessary documentation for tax returns, financial statements, and valuations, plus they help the team find solutions that result in the lowest tax outlay. They also can have business consulting practices that can provide extensive assistance in numerous areas of running a business.

Financial Advisors

Financial advisors, comprising wealth managers, private bankers, and financial planners, play a critical role as part of any well-rounded BHBO advisory team. In addition to financial planning, investment management, financial modeling, and access to financial markets, many financial advisors are experienced in subject areas that are important to you and your business: succession planning, asset protection, estate planning, corporate retirement programs, and taxes. It is also not at all uncommon for financial advisors to act in a coaching capacity or even have psychologists in their practices to help deal with the many emotional aspects of family wealth.

Depending on the type of practice they pursue, financial advisors sometimes have a slightly easier path to certification and specialization than attorneys and CPAs do. However, they operate under several organizations that oversee one of the most heavily regulated industries in the country. These include the Financial Industry Regulatory Authority (FINRA), the Securities and Exchange Commission (SEC), the Department of Labor (DOL), the National Association of Insurance Commissioners (NAIC), and each state's financial service department of securities and insurance.

On the individual level, financial advisors have several possible paths to certification. Series 7 is the difficult broker exam, highlighted in such movies as *The Pursuit of Happyness,* typically required by large firms such as Merrill and Morgan Stanley. Other licenses are Series 65 and Series 6. Here's a quick overview of each:

- **Series 7** allows the representative to buy and sell stocks, bonds, mutual funds, and options for a commission.
- **Series 65** allows the advisor to charge a fee to manage financial portfolios and offer financial advice. The recently enacted "Regulation BI" prohibits representatives from using the term *advisor* unless they have passed the Series 65 exam.
- **Series 6** allows the representative to sell mutual funds or insurance products with mutual fund options.

Much like CPAs and attorneys, financial advisors also have many areas of specialization. They can focus on the needs of a business owner, nonprofit, 401(k), retiree, divorce, corporate client, and so forth. As the Series exams cover little in the way of taxes, asset protection, retirement plans, and exit strategies, it is very important to ensure your advisor has had experience in the area you need advisement. Many large financial services firms, like Merrill Lynch, Raymond James, UBS, and Edward Jones, offer additional training programs to their advisors in specific areas of specialization, such as taxes, asset protection, and succession planning.

While an advisor with significant experience can be a tremendous help without these specializations, additional professional designations are a good sign of professional competency and commitment to excellence. Additionally, most designations require recipients to follow strict codes of ethics. Following is a partial list of useful designations to consider:

- **CFP®:** Managed by the CFP Board, the CERTIFIED FINANCIAL PLANNER™ designation is one of the most recognized and difficult designations in the industry. It includes many subject areas such as tax, estate planning, succession, investing, and retirement planning.
- **CPWA®:** The Certified Private Wealth Advisor® is a designation covering topics similar to those of the CFP® but focused more on high–net worth issues and issued by a separate entity, the Investment and Wealth Institute.
- **AIF®** (Accredited Investment Fiduciary by Center for Fiduciary Studies) and **CRPS®** (Chartered Retirement Plans Specialist by the College for Financial Planning): Designations specific to corporate retirement plans.

Since your financial advisor will be managing your money, there are a few important designations to consider that demonstrate skill: a Certified Financial Analyst (CFA®) is a four-year program focused on securities analysis and money management, and a Certified Investment Management Analyst (CIMA®) is a one-year program that focuses on port-folio construction for pools of money like family offices, en-dowments, foundations, and retirement plans. Certainly, there are other worthwhile designations, and it is worth your time to explore the topics covered and the academic rigor of the designation. I encourage you to ask potential advisors about their training, experience, and designations when interviewing them for your team. Get references and check the FINRA and SEC websites to see if an advisor has proper credentialing and if they have a history of any disciplinary action.

Bankers

No business can survive without adequate cash to meet its obligations, which is why a banker is a critical business advi-sor to have on your BHBO team. Bankers ensure that cash is available when needed. Additionally, among the sources of corporate financing available to business owners when needed, bank loans typically offer the lowest interest rates and thus the cheapest cost of capital.

Even though interest rates are currently extremely low, bankers can also help with many forms of cash management to sometimes squeeze more income out of working capital. They can also sometimes help with some sophisticated tools in merchant services and payroll.

While commercial bankers do not need to pass any par-ticular exams, the vast majority of banks only hire bankers with some financial background—for example, degrees in finance or accounting, or MBAs. Here, again, experience is key. You want to work with a banker who understands your line of business and your financial statements and who has the interpersonal skills to be your advocate when you need a loan. One of the best sources of information on bankers comes from referrals from others. Look for bankers who have a good combination of industry knowledge, customer service, and business advocacy.

While most compensation for bankers is usually a salary and bonus structure, internal incentives for bankers can vary dramatically. Certainly, a salary with a bonus based on the banker's ability to close loans on your behalf can closely align their interests with yours.

Insurance Professionals

If nothing ever went wrong, we wouldn't need insurance or insurance professionals. Unfortunately, life doesn't work that way, so insurance is another critical aspect of managing the risks of running a business. As a business owner, you will constantly juggle the risks you are willing to accept and the risks you want to insure. While it may be appropriate for you to have multiple experts in each category (e.g., a corporate attorney and a tax attorney), it is especially important to have specialists in the insurance field, as each is quite different, and the licenses required to offer coverage rarely require holders to show competencies in the important areas you need as a business owner. For instance, the life and health insurance license does not cover product knowledge, whereas an experienced group health specialist would know the companies and products best suited to the health issues and financial acumen of your workforce.

Insurance is a highly sophisticated tool used to transfer risk, and a good agent can be a tremendous help not only in helping find a cost-effective product for the risk you do not want to accept (or are required to purchase—like medical malpractice, unemployment, or directors and officers coverage), but they can also help you with ideas that reduce your risk without insurance. I have watched skilled casualty agents work with employers to implement risk-management programs that not only helped protect workers but also reduced costs dramatically. Many are also skilled in helping to evaluate tools such as captive insurance companies, which allow the business owner to establish their own "private" insurance company to potentially gain underwriting profits if claims are low.

Insurance licensing generally is offered in two categories: life/health and property/casualty. The National Association of Insurance Commissioners (NAIC) sets guidelines and standards, but licensing and regulation are handled by each state. The licensing of insurance agents generally takes less time than that of advisors in the securities business, so make sure your agent has experience in the area servicing your business. It is common for agents to specialize in one of four categories: life insurance, health insurance, individual property-casualty, and business property casualty.

Much like financial advisors, an array of professional designations demonstrates competence and the pursuit of excellence in various areas. For those in property-casualty insurance, the designation most recognized is the CPCU® (Chartered Property & Casualty Underwriter by the American Institute for Chartered Property & Casualty Underwriters). The designation typically takes two to three years to complete and covers a wide range of risk management topics focused on business and personal casualty/liability risk.

The main life insurance designation is the CLU® (Chartered Life Underwriter by the American College of Financial Services). This designation covers such topics as estate planning, life insurance products (which are quite complicated), estate taxes, and succession planning. A life insurance agent with significant experience is typically well versed in these areas even without the designation. As these are highly technical areas, it is not uncommon for some life insurance agents to build out a wealth management practice to concentrate on their additional skills.

The designation most common for the group health specialist is the REBC® (Registered Employee Benefits Consultant by the National Association of Health Underwriters). Especially with the growing cost of health coverage and the ever-changing regulatory landscape after the passage of the Affordable Care Act, having a guide is critical. I have also seen human resource managers become health agents, bringing their experience and advice with multiple human resource issues to the table. These professionals sometimes earn the SHRM®-CP or SHRM®-SCP (Society of Human Resource Professionals-Certified Professional or Senior Certified Professional), which is certainly a worthwhile designation if you have employees within your human resource department.

Investment Bankers and Business Brokers

If you plan to eventually sell your business to an outside party or wish to purchase a business, an investment banker or business broker (sometimes called intermediaries) can be a valuable addition to your advisory team. Investment bankers are also key advisors for business owners who wish to sell public or private debt or equity. In addition to assisting with sale and purchase transactions, a good investment banker or business broker can also help you see how your past or future business decisions might be viewed in such transactions or by financial markets. Having a long-term relationship with an investment banker or business broker can help you chart the course for your business in the context of building value for eventual sale.

As a business sale or purchase is likely the largest and most stressful financial transaction you will ever undertake, an experienced intermediary can be invaluable in helping set reasonable expectations and ultimately getting the transaction to the closing table. Intermediaries can help with the estimation of your business's value, advise on growing your business, and help you acquire new businesses.

The licensing for business brokers varies by state; only about fifteen states currently require a license, though all states require a real estate license to sell any real estate that is part of a business transaction. With such a low barrier to entry, most business broker firms require their agents to have a business-related degree so they can understand the complicated financial transactions involved. Investment banking requires additional licensing, primarily the Series 79 from FINRA, which allows bankers to offer advice or facilitate offerings of public or private debt or equity. Most compensation comes from commissions on the sale of a business or property or on fundraising to accomplish a transaction.

Consultants

What is a current pain point in your business? It's likely there is a consultant who can help you fix the problem and help take a business to the next level. I believe three things should be in place before your hire a consultant:

1. You have a reasonably well-defined difficulty or opportunity.
2. Your consultant has the experience and financial motivation to assist you in enacting the changes that need to be made.
3. You or your team have time to make sure the suggested changes become a new habit.

Good business consultants may be retired business owners or trained professionals within their industry, but it is critically important they have relevant experience in your industry.

Consultants who can have the greatest impact on your business focus on leadership, teamwork, sales development, financial operations, and technology. Compensation for consultants varies dramatically, from hourly fees, project fees, commissions, performance-based fees, and more. I would simply advise trying to align their compensation with the success of whatever project you are pursuing.

Peer Groups

It can be quite lonely at the top, as it is typically not appropriate to discuss challenges with employees. A formal group of CEO peers can share valuable insights, as they are likely to have faced many of the same challenges. Many such groups are well organized, with topics chosen to generate thought-provoking discussions, provide resources that other CEOs have found helpful, and offer seminars from speakers on a wide variety of topics. As a past member of Vistage, I have become a believer in the power of peer groups; they have helped me in many ways, including encouraging me to write this book! CEO peers are uniquely positioned to help business owners navigate the many challenges of ownership.

How Should You Manage Your Team?

Once you have decided on the unique mix of advisors that you need for the journey to your destination and completed the selection process for specific advisors, it's time to start managing your new team. How do you get the most out of each advisor, capitalize on the wisdom of the group, and create a cohesive and effective communication system for your team? Here are some of the best practices that I share with my clients:

- **Start with an introductory process**. For people to work well together, they need to build rapport and trust. A great head start on this process for a new team is a lunch or other social activity to get to know one another. No business needs to be discussed, as such meetings are meant to build rapport among those who will be working for your benefit.

- **Appoint a head air traffic controller**. Though you should have a direct relationship with all your advisors, you should appoint one to take the lead—to be your team's organizer. This advisor will be asked to help create agendas and take notes to help make sure the team stays on task. How do you pick the head air traffic controller? You need someone who will ask proactive questions, source ideas, and help coordinate your advisory team to implement those ideas. Most of the time this air traffic controller is your financial advisor or accountant, though any team member with the right characteristics can fill the role.

- **Clearly articulate all goals**. In your initial business meeting and in all those that follow, it is good to have a few goals outlined in an agenda. It need not be lengthy, just something to keep the team on track. We also like to provide a one-page mind map outlining your long-term goals, values, big-picture balance sheet, family members, legal structures, and team members. It is a great way to remind everyone (sometimes even yourself) about your planning situation, especially as your situation becomes more complicated. I have included a sample of the resources on my website.

- **Tie all goals to a timeline**. If there are no deadlines, it is unlikely that tasks will be completed promptly. You and your advisors are busy people; make sure everyone knows when things are due.

- **Create clear communication channels.** What are the best channels of communication for you and your team members? Discuss this important point and then articulate it clearly in the channels of communications—both how and to whom. This is most important when you and your team decide a project or idea is worth pursuing. You might instruct everyone to email the appointed air traffic controller once a month with updates, which can then be presented to you in a digest format. Or you could similarly appoint your CFO or executive assistant to follow up.

- **Discuss how accountability will be handled.** Over twenty-five years, I don't recall one instance where a team member shirked accountability or in which potential conflicts were not easily managed. If you have chosen your team well, advisors thrive in this type of team environment. But if rules do need to be made, these apply:

  1. The business owner is always in charge.
  2. See rule 1.

- **Host an annual summit.** One of the most powerful and simple tools for bringing the collective talents of your team together is a summit. A summit brings your core advisory team into the same room to prepare and discuss ways to improve your position based on your personal and business goals. Usually, it's helpful to have the head air traffic controller coordinate the agenda, but most of the time I've found these meetings take on a life of their own and generate ideas nobody would have considered before. A summit doesn't need to take place annually, nor does it need to be lengthy—one to two hours is usually enough unless a particular project or challenge is pressing on your mind.

Family Offices and Private Wealth

Larger family businesses sometimes keep some or all of their advisory team members on the payroll in the form of a family office. This means that advisors—particularly the financial advisor, accountant, and attorney—are employed by the family (on retainer, on some fee basis, or as outright employees) and answer only to the family. This structure can have the benefit of making sure advisors know the family well and are 100 percent committed to its well-being. Sometimes a family office evolves naturally as wealth grows, or sometimes it is created deliberately after a large exit or liquidity event. In some cases, a limited number of families can share the same team. The term *private wealth* is usually synonymous with comprehensive planning for high–net worth (HNW) individuals and are specialized groups of advisors within banks, broker-dealer firms, or independent financial advisory firms.

How Can You Avoid Bad Actors?

Years ago, in my hometown of Charleston, South Carolina, there was a local economist named Al Parish, who managed to entice several individuals to invest millions of their hard-earned dollars with him. Parish called himself Economan, and he gave regular speeches at local Chamber of Commerce events. He invested these monies in collectibles (notably, pens and artwork), then created statements with unverified assumptions showing impressive returns. He drove a Jaguar with a leopard-patterned soft top. After years of gaining clients, Parish was arrested and pleaded guilty to financial fraud. He was sentenced to twenty-four years in prison. Unfortunately, investors only recovered a fraction of their initial investments. Did Parish have licenses to conduct this business? A review of either of the FINRA and SEC sites would have revealed that he did not possess such licenses. I believe such a review of his background would have triggered a deeper exploration into his infrastructure and potentially could have saved many from this unfortunate financial loss.

The reality is that almost every industry has a small number of bad actors, and you need a process to sniff them out before you ask them to join your BHBO advisory board. As a business owner, you undoubtedly realize the importance of screening good employees to contribute to the business and make the work environment more enjoyable. You need a similar screen for your advisors. Verify they are properly credentialed and have the background you expect.

Your Air Traffic Controllers Are Manning their Stations!

Before every commercial flight, pilots have set their destination (goals), check the weather and plot their path (completed planning), file a flight plan (shared plan with air traffic controllers [ATCs]), and check their compass to be sure it operates properly (mission statement). When on the ground before takeoff, they talk to ATC to receive a clearance—which may share small adjustments to their flight plan depending on weather or traffic. ATC is ready, and they are almost ready to take off! In the next few chapters I will discuss understanding the instruments that will help guide the journey, the checklists to help with normal business operations, understanding the type of plane you are flying, and finally understanding the emergency checklists and procedures needed to help keep you and your passengers safe as you journey toward your destination.

Chapter 4

Keeping Personal and Business Goals Aligned and On Course

— — — — — — — — — —

"WITHOUT DREAMS AND GOALS THERE IS NO LIVING, ONLY MERELY EXISTING, AND THAT IS NOT WHY WE ARE HERE."
—MARK TWAIN

Pilots learn early that the inner ear can play tricks on the mind while flying. With clouds blocking their sightline, a pilot can experience vertigo. For example, a pilot may think they are climbing to the right when they are descending to the left. This dangerous disorientation can lead to poor decision-making and unfortunate outcomes. To avoid this, pilots must learn to trust their instruments, which provide the type of reliable information they need to make the right decisions. Additionally, these instruments allow pilots to monitor the health of their aircraft to avoid problems before they occur.

Similarly, BHBOs need reliable information to navigate the long journey to their goals. What are the proper instruments for a BHBO? I will discuss many in this chapter, but I believe one of the most important instruments to help align the personal and business goals and stay on course is a financial plan that incorporates the use of the business—a business owner financial plan.

Business Owner Financial Plan

Goal setting usually comes naturally for business owners. Aligning personal goals with business goals doesn't always feel as natural. This is not surprising given that business owners are trained to separate every aspect of their personal and business lives—accounting, legal, financing, management, and even strategic vision. This separation is critical for legal and financial compliance as well as to minimize liability. When it comes to a BHBO's goals, however, the opposite is true. Business owners must have a very different mindset when it comes to goals. Personal and business goals must be closely aligned for BHBOs who wish to reach their destination while being aligned with their compass. Consider the following:

- Early on in a company's life cycle, it is not uncommon for business owners to utilize their personal balance sheets to fund their business. How does this funding affect a business owner's personal goals? How does it accelerate business success, and when and how does that success support a BHBO's personal goals?
- How do a BHBO's personal goals influence the type of business that is being built? Is there a specific corporate structure that can support a faster journey toward a BHBO's destination?
- How does the business's exit strategy impact the business owner's personal goals? Does the exit strategy seek maximum value? Does it maintain a profitable business for the next generation of family or employees? Does it strive to maintain

a certain corporate culture? Does it provide the BHBO with enough money to fund their family's lifestyle while still being able to accomplish charitable goals?

- How much of your business's profits should be distributed to meet personal goals, and what are the most tax-efficient means of distributing those profits?

A business owner's financial plan can help owners see the big picture of how their personal balance sheet, the business balance sheet, and their goals can intersect. All good financial plans should be holistic in their approach, but many financial plans have a narrow focus and offer only a few tools in general areas like retirement, education, and estate planning. Tools like retirement plans, IRAs, 529 plans, and mortgages are probably familiar to you. The financial plan of a BHBO has far more moving parts:

- The business—usually the largest asset and source of goal funding
- Real estate, not just for the business but perhaps as part of an investment portfolio
- Retirement programs unique to owners, such as stock options: nonqualified plans or buy/sell agreements
- Debts unique to the business that may include a personal guarantee.

A BHBO might have additional assets, tax write-offs, and other considerations that make their financial scenario even more complex. Any financial plan for a BHBO should include the owner's unique charitable goals, legacy goals, and family- and employee-care goals. These issues are far more complex than the typical financial plan can accommodate. A good financial plan allows the owner and their team to see how all these parts of the corporate and personal balance sheet affect one another. This will allow the BHBO's team to efficiently navigate toward an optimal outcome toward the BHBO's destination.

Following are important fundamental components of an effective business owner financial plan:

The ability to separate lifestyle goals from aspirational goals. Lifestyle goals include items like retirement income, college funding, travel, personal real estate, and family gifting. Aspirational goals are things like charitable gifting, legacy/estate planning, starting additional businesses, or other items important for the BHBO but not necessarily related to funding their lifestyle.

The ability to model many sophisticated assets, liabilities, and tax consequences. This type of modeling is crucial to assess the outcomes for handling numerous aspects of the portfolio in different ways. Taxation of investment real estate, different types of business exits, nonqualified deferred compensation, corporate loans, and stock options are just a few of the elements that must be included in the model for BHBOs.

The ability to isolate a few important variables to help show the impact of important decisions. Because there are so many moving parts in a business owner's portfolio, a good plan can show the impact of different forms of exits, different timing for the exit, different. taxation rates in specific states, or even potential modeling of purchase scenarios with expected returns to show how they affect goals.

The objective is to use the plan as an ongoing tool to help you and the team better view the potential outcomes of important decisions throughout your life: from operating a business with a young family to deciding on an exit strategy, to making decisions through retirement after business assets are converted to financial assets. Many business owners focus strictly on the return on investment (ROI), but what about the idea of focusing on the ROG—or return on goals?

Consider the following two exit stories—one without a financial plan, the other with:

> Bob was 50 with a young family and a small florist business. The business cleared approximately $500,000 in annual earnings—remarkable for the size of the business. Normally a business of this size might command three to five times EBITDA (earnings before income taxes, depreciation, and amortization). So, when a chain looking to move into the area offered $3.5 million cash for the business, Bob was super excited and sold it as soon as the details were finalized. It was not a bad day for Bob. However, after spending some of this money as a personal reward, paying taxes, and paying off the house, Bob had only $2 million left. From the perspective of today's low interest rate environment, a 3.8 percent yield would net his family only about $72,000 per year—hardly enough to fund the lifestyle they had built around their business, let alone allow them to achieve their legacy goals. Even though Bob started another business after the sale, he wondered if he should have kept the business longer as a way of building his personal net worth. A financial plan would have shown that even though he received top dollar for the business, it probably was too early for him to sell.

> David was 65, lived a relatively modest lifestyle, and was very active with his church and missions. With a grown family, a few grandchildren, and a balance sheet including a modest amount of real estate and retirement tools, his financial plan told him they needed approximately $3 million more to fund his family's lifestyle and aspirational goals. As he evaluated his options, which included sale to an outside party versus a management buyout through an ESOP (employee stock ownership plan), he realized each option would likely have a different purchase price—the outside sale being the highest, estimated at $5.5 million. He ultimately chose an ESOP with

the lower purchase price of $4.5 million because he would pay far fewer taxes on this sale. The ESOP would also allow him to maintain the culture of his business and make decisions about when he would stop working in the business. Because of the tax savings, he would still have enough money to make a $500,000 gift to his favorite charity. As this gift was made before the sale, it helped save capital gains taxes on the gift, saving around $100,000 capital gains taxes in addition to the savings from the $500,000 tax deduction. Without a financial plan, David would not have understood that the lower purchase price of the ESOP afforded him a higher ROG because it was sufficient to fund his family's lifestyle while also keeping an eye out for his important charitable goals. I have included a sample business owner retirement plan on my website.

Important Corporate Instruments

As business management guru Peter Drucker once said, "If you can't measure it, you can't improve it." Many management books are written on the topic of creating and reading financial statements as a business owner, which are easy to find with a little research. Whether they are prepared by your CFO, a bookkeeper, your CPA, or you like to create them yourself, watching your financials is critically important to be sure you have ample liquidity, you can limit financial surprises, and you can take advantage of opportunities as they appear. Financial statements are also critical to your ability to obtain and maintain bank financing, making them a core instrument to be tracked regularly.

Unique to each business are also key performance indicators (KPIs) that measure their business's growth and financial health. Different types of businesses have different KPIs. For example, a consulting company or law firm might measure success against billable hours. A manufacturer would watch the number of products purchased each month and inventory controls. A software company might measure churn—the number of new subscribers versus those lost. Whatever your business, you should be measuring several KPIs to ensure your business is healthy and growing.

There are a few KPIs that all businesses share. These are the basics of financial well-being. While you want to find the best KPIs for your company and industry, the following are a few basic KPIs that I believe are essential for any business:

- **Working capital**—Pilots know it's important to keep an eye on their fuel gauge. If it drops near zero, the engine will shut down, forcing an immediate landing. Working capital for the business owner is equivalent to the fuel gauge; it measures whether a company has adequate liquidity. Working capital may be measured in several ways, depending on the cash needs of the business. One common measurement is the current ratio—that is, current assets divided by current liabilities. The ratio should almost always be greater than one or the business may be in trouble.
- **Revenue growth**—This KPI is the equivalent of an airplane's vertical speed indicator, which shows the rate of the plane's climb or descent. A positive rate of growth can confirm the business is doing well. A negative or flat rate of revenue growth may indicate a company is in trouble. However, it is important to compare this trend to overall industry trends to see how you're performing versus peers in different market cycles.
- **Margin**—Pilots watch fuel-flow indicators to show how fast they are burning fuel. In the same way, business owners must watch margins. If product lines, consulting engagements, or other sources of revenue are not generating a healthy margin, then profitability is an issue. Low margins ultimately have a negative impact on working capital. Maintaining adequate margins on most (if not all) lines of business is critical to success.

It is useful to note that with the application of artificial intelligence to financial services and the involvement of big players like Amazon

Web Services to business data, consider exploring services specific to your industry that create dashboards and track a fully customized set of KPIs. If you have large data sets to analyze (including, most obviously, financial statements), you will likely find a service that helps to convert that data into actionable information. A search for "KPI dashboard" in your industry is likely to show many options.

Next, I'll discuss other documents that can help keep your personal and business goals on track.

Important Personal Instruments

Happily, there are far fewer personal documents to keep organized than business documents. As a business owner, it is likely you regularly maintain personal financial statements when applying for bank loans. Having a clear picture on your personal balance sheet through these financial statements is critically important so that you have the capability of seizing on opportunities as they occur. Many banks and financial institutions today also have account aggregation services, which allow you to see all your financial holdings with current values in one spot. A good financial plan will update this information, ideally through automation.

A credit report is a frequently overlooked item that can sneak up on an owner if they are not careful. I have seen several business owners blindsided after applying for important business credit only to uncover an old, obscure past-due bill cratered their credit and either prevented a loan or forced less favorable terms. Even a small medical bill you thought incorrect can, unfortunately, have this effect on your credit score and should be managed. You can get a copy directly from the credit-reporting agencies (Experian, TransUnion, and Equifax) or through free credit-monitoring services offered by your bank or credit card company. It is important to check regularly, and long before needing credit, as it can take a while for scores to increase after paying off a past due bill.

Also, beware of maxing out your credit cards. This common trap might be the fastest way to hurt your credit, as the reporting agencies consider credit utilization high in determining your score. During the financial crisis of 2008, many banks unilaterally reduced credit limits to the amount drawn, which immediately caused thousands of credit cards to be maxed out and hurt the credit scores of many, even though these individuals had never missed a payment and hadn't borrowed any more. At the same time, paying off high balances is one of the quickest ways to help your credit. I discuss some of the pros and cons of using credit cards as a source of business funding in the next chapter but suffice to say for now that credit cards should usually not be used for nonrecurring large projects; it will probably negatively affect your utilization and credit score.

Finally, monitoring your credit can help protect you against identity theft. The most common form of identity theft is someone using your name to apply for credit cards, rapidly maxing out the card usage, and then disappearing. This can quickly damage anyone's credit and can take a while to sort out if unnoticed. By using a credit-monitoring service, you can be alerted to such issues when they occur.

Checklists: The Benefits of Organization

Pilots love checklists. In aviation, since forgetting seemingly insignificant items can be devastating, there are checklists for every phase of flight: preflight, start-up, takeoff, post takeoff, cruise, before landing, after landing, and shutdown. There are also emergency checklists for as many conceivable emergencies as possible. It can be said pilots don't tie their shoelaces without a checklist! For the BHBO, these standard operating checklists can be crucial for the different phases of their flight. I'm going to assume that if you're reading this book, you know how to read basic business documents. Thus, I will focus on the importance of having these documents organized and highlight some that I believe are particularly useful as checklists to keep the flight on path.

Having certain information and documents organized, current, and carefully tracked can not only help business owners stay reliably on course but also help them take advantage of opportunities as they happen. For instance, any business acquisition, buying or selling, requires a substantial set of documents during a process known as due diligence (I've included a sample on my website). Having these documents available and current not only helps accelerate the due diligence process for both buyers and sellers but can also meaningfully increase your selling price as the buyer realizes you run a tight ship. Countless business deals fall through when due diligence either turns up negative information or is so disorganized as to be unreliable.

The documents for personal organization may be considerably simpler, but no less important. The benefits to the BHBO are similar, in that they allow the owner to take advantage of opportunities as they arise. For instance, the opportunity to purchase property, equipment, or other businesses will likely depend on the strength of a business owner's personal balance sheet. Those organized and capable of pouncing on these opportunities reap many benefits from their focus on organization.

Since you are probably pressed for time, it can be incredibly useful to enlist your financial advisor, your attorney, employees (CFO/accounting), or a separate group to archive and track important financial documents. Creating organization upfront makes it easier to access documents when you need them and dramatically improves the closing process when you finally sell your business. Here are the types of documents that you should have organized and used as your checklists:

Corporate books. Owning a business through a corporate entity (whether an LLC, S Corp, or C Corp) can help shield its owners from liabilities arising from business activities. However, a company should act like a company, or the legal system can break through this asset protection. Such corporate governance is an important part of running and exiting a business.

The corporate books are the main documents that demonstrate good corporate governance. Comprising the checklists on how decisions should be made, these documents should be reviewed by attorneys periodically to be sure all are current and in order; this will help prevent problems from compounding down the road.

The corporate books vary depending on the type of corporation and the state of domicile. Generally speaking, S or C corporations will have articles of incorporation along with corporate bylaws as the governing documents, whereas an LLC will have an operating agreement. These documents help outline the protocols for making important decisions, including election and term of officers, the purchase and sale of stock, the establishment of committees, the provision of corporate employee benefits, and other items you and your attorney believe are important to your company.

An important part of corporate books, "minutes" document when, where, and by whom important decisions about the company are made during corporate meetings. While smaller companies may not have the full parliamentary formality of regular board meetings, documenting decision-making through meeting minutes that reflect the conversations of those with voting interest is still critically important. As the company and number of shareholders grow, it is essential to conduct more formal meetings using parliamentary procedures discussing and documenting corporate affairs. Follow the advice of your attorney.

Human resource documents. These include your employment agreements, human resources manuals, and documentation surrounding your employee benefits programs. All provide your company's rules around hiring, firing, management, and benefits. As employees are a company's most valuable asset, these documents help you to not just set policy but actively craft ways to take care of your employees and keep them happy and productive.

Unfortunately, not following these checklists can have catastrophic consequences. For instance, failure to follow plan documents or not supervising a retirement plan can subject the owner to personal liability. This is because retirement plan laws (ERISA—the Employee Retirement Income Security Act of 1974 governing retirement plans) specifically void corporate asset protection for poor governance of retirement plans. You may have generous match and profit-sharing contributions, but missing items like treating employees differently for loans, delaying submitting employee deferral, failing to oversee the fund lineup, or not following documents as they are written can all result in Department of Labor penalties or personal liability. Thus, it is critical to review these checklists regularly. Larger companies will typically hire a human resources director to ensure compliance while smaller companies may outsource some of their HR to outside professionals (retirement or health specialists) or professional employer organizations (PEOs) until they reach a certain size. The Pension Protection Act of 2019 also made it easier to outsource retirement tasks to multiple employer plans or pooled employer plans to simplify administration and share or reduce your liability. It's also important to have adequate insurance coverage in this area. Business owners can easily run afoul of rules and pay disproportionate penalties despite their good intentions. Having a good team—with either internal or external benefits specialists—is critical.

Business plan. This can be a much more enjoyable topic of conversation for many business owners! It helps highlight the strategy you have for growing the business and is typically reviewed and rewritten at least annually. The one unique part of this planning for the BHBO is the importance of reviewing the company mission statement (as will be discussed in the next chapter). An up-to-date business plan helps the BHBO convert the mission to numbers and execution. Although owners understand business planning well, I have seen many find it helpful to employ Jim Collins's concept of the flywheel, as described in his book *Turning the Flywheel.* The idea is to distill the essence of your business's success into a diagram to help continue growth. A quick Internet search for "flywheel" will produce many diagrams, including Amazon's famous and much-discussed version.

Instruments and Checklists to Prepare for the Worst and Hope for Best

Back in World War II, the US Air Force provided supplies to China as it fought Japan by ferrying supplies from India over the Eastern Himalayas. One stretch of the mountains was particularly treacherous, reaching heights up to 15,000 feet and earning the nickname "The Hump." Normal propeller airplanes become far less efficient at high altitudes. The thin air makes it more difficult for their engines to provide power to

Some Instruments for Private Equity Held Companies

Not every business is destined to be partners, recipients of funding, or acquired entities of institutional buyers, such as what you might see on the TV show *Shark Tank.* A well-managed business that grows and becomes profitable with nothing more than bank financing nearly always gives the owner the most amount of control. Focusing on profitability and growth with no need for outside help can also help drive higher valuations. However, the potentially lucrative space of private equity has its own set of financial lingo/instruments that should be understood if you are building a scalable business with the intention of using this route for a future liquidity event. One of the best books I've read on the topic is *Venture Deals: Be Smarter Than Your Lawyer and Venture Capitalist.* Following is a non-comprehensive primer of terms used for businesses involved in software, which also can be taken from corporate financial statements and customized.

- **ARR**—Annualized run rate, commonly used for rapidly growing businesses. Projects a given the propellers. Add the weight of loaded cargo, and it is little wonder why pilots dreaded flying over The Hump. Many crews were lost in WWII when the aircraft could not overfly the mountain tops. Only crews with the proper weight, balance, timing relative to weather, maintenance, attention to their checklists and instruments—and a little luck—were able to make it across The Hump without incident. It required planning for a worst-case scenario and tremendous diligence, skill, and courage. Those pilots who successfully navigated their cargo over The Hump enjoyed relatively smooth sailing for the remainder of their flight.

Nearly every business and business owner experiences "humps" sooner or later: The business might run into cash flow difficulties as it tries to fund growth and fulfill growing orders. Maybe the business loses a key customer or employee to a competitor. Look at what the pandemic did to companies around the world in 2020. There are a million potential scenarios, but in each case, the business owner must fully understand the challenges as well as the instruments and checklists necessary to navigate the business

period's gross revenue (typically monthly) into the annualized amount.

- **Customer acquisition cost**—Deeper within more detailed portions of financial statements, it isolates the cost to acquire one customer.
- **Customer lifetime value**—Usually involving some projections, this is an estimate of the average annual revenue times average years as a client.
- **LTV/CAC (customer lifetime value/customer acquisition cost)**—This is a ratio of the previous two metrics showing a signal of customer profitability and sales/marketing efficiency.
- **Dollar revenue retention**—This shows the number of recurring revenues.

Another set of instruments unique to private equity is what is commonly called a capitalization (or cap) table. These outline the number and type of shareholders for a business (I've included a sample on my website). Most BHBOs have simple ownership structures with only a handful of owners. These types over the inevitable hump and into smoother skies. Watching the instruments and following the checklists are critical, or your business may not make it over.

As a pilot, the most enjoyable part of flying is the actual manual input into the controls to make the airplane do your bidding—what is called "stick and rudder" flying, just you, the airplane, and nature in a three-dimensional dance with the clouds. When I was an instructor, I would usually cover the instruments with sticky notes to force them to focus on the look and feel of piloting the aircraft through multiple configurations without help from instruments. That way they can see the look of the horizon, the sound of the airflow, and the sensations in the seat of their pants as they controlled the aircraft. However, stick and rudder flying does not work in the clouds by itself. It doesn't work by itself when you are trying to fly to a specific destination. For both, you need to use your instruments.

of businesses have little need for a process in tracking owners. However, it is common through multiple funding rounds (angel, Series A, Series B, etc.) that there are dozens or even hundreds of owners with different terms of ownership. A cap table can help quickly show the structure and can have a bearing on the overall value for future investors. It can become exceedingly complex. Happily, several companies can assist in tracking ownership and shares for businesses along with document signing, valuation, and other useful services for growing businesses with multiple funding "rounds." It is critically important to document this process early, as making mistakes regarding your shareholder's ownership rights can be devastating to both the business and the investor. While there may be many others, the following are a few services to explore in your search: Carta, Capshare, or Shareworks.

Chapter 5

Is Your Business A fighter JET, A cargo PLANE, or A hybrid?

━ ━ ━ ━ ━ ━ ━ ━ ━ ━

"IF YOU SCREW UP..... YOU'LL BE FLYING A CARGO PLANE
FULL OF RUBBER DOG SHIT OUT OF HONG KONG."
—STINGER, TOP GUN

As a child of the 80s, the movie *Top Gun* inspired me (and many others) to pursue a career strapped into a fighter "going Mach 2 with my hair on fire." It's what prompted me to enroll in Purdue's Aeronautical Engineer program. Years later, a failed eye exam would force me to pursue a different career, which has been wonderful. Fighter jets are exciting aircrafts, built for speed, maneuverability, armament, and resiliency. And though Stinger's quote pokes fun at cargo planes, they can be just as exhilarating and are certainly just as important for the defense of our country. Many of my friends who flew C17 cargo planes out of my hometown of Charleston have shared cool stories about dropping their planes from 40,000 feet in the dark of night without lights right into a combat zone—all in a matter of minutes. Even in a cargo plane, flying can be a thrill ride. No matter what they fly, pilots love their planes. So, what do fighter jets and cargo planes have to do with financial planning and your true north? More than you might think.

Fighter and cargo planes are perfect analogies for the two main types of businesses (broadly speaking). Growth-oriented and scalable businesses are like fighter planes. They are typically disruptive and built on new technology or offer a new way of doing things. They need to be nimble to actively shoot down the competition and gain rapid traction and growth. The other type is income-oriented businesses. Found mainly in well-established service sectors, they are the cargo planes of the business world. They don't necessarily need to be able to shoot down the competition. Success for this type of company requires efficiency to generate a healthy income. Finally, there's the hybrid: a business that has the characteristics of growth and income businesses. They may be a service business that is scalable or a technology business with high income from a service channel.

Just as pilots need to understand what type of plane they are flying, business owners need to understand what type of business they're running. Think about it: You wouldn't fly a cargo plane into a battle zone; it's too big and slow. It would be an easy target. It's not the right type of plane for that assignment. Conversely, you wouldn't fly a fighter jet across the ocean with a bunch of soldiers and supplies stuffed tightly into its small cargo hold. Each airplane model is designed for a different type of mission. Some are built for distance, some for speed, some for capacity, and so on. A pilot flying the wrong type of plane is unlikely to fulfill their duties effectively or successfully. The same is true of BHBOs.

Each type of business has different cash needs, scalability challenges, growth trajectories, taxation ramifications, and exit strategies. Planning for these areas in ways that are appropriate to each business type is critically important, so let's dive into some specifics. Following are the most common characteristics and trajectories of income/cargo plane, growth/fighter jet, and hybrid businesses. I'll also discuss some of the unique needs of family businesses.

The Cargo Plane: Stable Income Producers

If you're piloting a cargo plane style business, you will be familiar with some of its typical characteristics:

Lower growth. With this type of company, the capacity for growth is limited, especially if it's a service company. Common limitations include the number of hours staff are available to work and prices the market will bear.

High and consistent income. The hallmark of this type of business is that it generates higher and steadier income. This, in turn, provides options for the owner to add capacity (equipment/personnel), generate outside wealth, and support a comfortable lifestyle.

Low demand for capital. Even though every business needs some capital, especially at inception, a cargo business needs less outside capital because it generates revenue on its own. The irony is that banks love these types of businesses, as they can more easily identify an income stream or assets to secure loans.

Difficult to scale. It's not impossible to scale a cargo business but doing so does require the owner to deliberately counter natural business tendencies that rely heavily on the owner's expertise. For instance, the owner of an accounting or physician practice might have spent considerable time building a reputation that allows them to fill up their schedule and/or increase rates, but it is harder to transfer that reputation to other people to "scale" the business.

With this type of business, the BHBO meets their personal and professional goals through ongoing income generated by the business.

There is less reliance on (and typically less interest in) a liquidity event that provides a larger sum of cash upon the sale of the business.

As income producers, cargo businesses are typically service-oriented, sometimes run by licensed professionals that create a barrier to entry, such as specialized degrees, board certifications, or licenses. Doctors, dentists, lawyers, and accountants fall into this category. Higher cash flow is typically based on the expertise of the owner. Sometimes this expertise can be replicated to create branded services and correspondingly increase the customer base and net revenue—for example, trade businesses, large medical practices, and construction companies. However, this is the exception not the rule for these types of businesses.

These reliable, income-generating businesses typically experience the following trajectory:

> **Start-up phase.** The amount of cash needed to get the business off the ground is typically lower than a growth business since services do not usually need to fund significant start-up costs for equipment, product development, and other tasks requiring a heavy lift. In those cases, in which outside capital is needed, it is typically easier to obtain for an income business than it is for a growth business, as the lender normally considers it more likely they will be repaid. For instance, a medical practice may have quite a bit of start-up equipment, but lenders realize cash flow is likely to follow quickly.

> **Growth phase.** As long as the business attracts customers and maintains healthy margins, it can consistently grow the net free cash flow (cash flow minus all expenses) for stakeholders. This free cash flow can be maintained throughout the business cycle and can be used to either accelerate business growth or build net worth outside of the business.

> **Exit phase.** Depending on both the scalability of the business and the owner's level of expertise, exit values are usually

modest (lower multiple of free cash flow) compared to growth businesses. In some cases, such as with professional services, valuation can be as low as less than one year's revenue.

This type of business is very stable but can still face challenges. Here are a few:

Mixing personal and business expenses. Because of the naturally high income of this type of business, it's easy to have the business pay for personal expenses (cars, cell phones for family, trips). While certainly many expenses can be appropriately justified, owners must be very careful and rely on the expertise of their team to appropriately split expenses. Having them confused can not only hurt your business valuation but also be troublesome in the event of an IRS audit.

Spending too much before exit. Since exits for this type of business are typically at a lower valuation, business owners must build personal wealth in a tax-efficient manner long before an exit. It's also important for these owners to be strategic before the sale of their company. For example, those equipment purchases that provide tax deductions now can eat away at the business's free cash flow during the exit phase. This can make the business less attractive to buyers since it further reduces the business valuation.

Because of the lower exit valuation and higher cash flow, it is wise to orchestrate a strategy consistent with personal goals that either build net worth outside the business or works toward making the business less reliant on the owner in the successful operation of the business, which helps business be scalable to other markets. (I will discuss many tax-efficient ways to build worth outside the business for yourself and those you care about in chapter 7.)

The Fighter Jet: Faster, Riskier, and More Demanding

For the BHBO running this type of company, personal goals are more often met through a liquidity event than they are through earned income over time. These types of high-growth businesses are usually created because the founder had a new idea or a way to improve on an old idea. Software companies, biotech companies, and consumer goods with high demand fall into this category. They are the disrupters with high capital demands and a high potential for capital gains, but they are also high risk. This type of business generally has the following characteristics:

High growth. For this type of business, there is a strong potential to disrupt an existing industry, sometimes in a new business sector where fewer businesses have trodden. The higher growth comes when the business is discovered by its market and begins to experience traction—a common term for this high growth as the company stirs up high demand. Organic growth for income-oriented cargo businesses might be up to 20 percent annually, while a fast-growth fighter business could have an annual growth of 100 percent or more.

Demands a lot of capital. Higher demand for more products or services usually brings about a higher demand for capital to sustain the growth. This higher demand for capital brings about a higher risk along with the potential for a higher reward down the road. The reason for the added risk is that usually, the founder doesn't have the balance sheet to support high growth without seeking outside funding. Borrowing money to fund growth (leverage) and/or bringing in new investors (dilution) increase the overall risk of a business. If the business does not continue to grow to support the additional capital, the business can run into a significant cash crunch. On the other side of this risk is the potential return: The additional capital can help the company scale up to much higher valuations.

Scalable. This simply means the business can be replicated and rapidly build demand in larger and diversified markets.

As high-growth engines, these fighter jet businesses typically have multiple fits and starts—called pivots—in which the business model is adjusted until a market fit is established. It is much like a fighter jet in tight turns during air combat. These risky, fast-growing businesses typically experience the following trajectory:

Start-up phase. This phase usually starts with considerable funding from the owner or outside investors and takes a while before it begins to have a positive cash flow. The start-up phase can last several years until the business finds traction. During the start-up phase, the company needs adequate runway (funding) before its growth takes off.

Growth phase. Once customers find the business, this type of company can enjoy rapid growth if it secures the additional investments it needs to add capacity and scale the business through research and development, product, manufacturing, marketing, sales, and other points along the product cycle. Cash and access to cash remain important. Excess cash flow is usually used to fund higher growth, maintaining low profit margins.

Maturity phase. All businesses need to show a profit eventually. The maturity phase is where excess cash flow can drive profit margins rather than be used primarily for growth.

Exit phase. Growth business valuations differ dramatically depending on the power of the company's idea and whether it has protected its intellectual property. Other factors, like growth rates, the size of the market served, and free cash flow generated, impact the exit as well. However, the valuations are usually much higher for this type of business than they are for the income businesses. Some of the challenges owners of fighter jet businesses can experience include the following:

Burnout. Bootstrapping is a common and expected strategy for most start-ups. It helps the owner preserve cash as long as possible while the company works to find its market fit. However, it is important to dial up the income of the business to maintain your lifestyle and avoid burnout. A growing business benefits greatly from a refreshed owner. Your family may also have less patience than you in the eventual success of a bootstrapped business. A more balanced lifestyle can increase the runway your family is willing to provide.

Becoming overleveraged. Borrowing or taking on investors can provide leverage and help accelerate the growth of a disruptive company. However, if this leverage comes with a high interest rate or difficult terms, the leverage can backfire over time, especially if the company doesn't meet aggressive growth rate goals. High interest rates can create a debt trap for the business, where interest on the debt is so high that it eats up profits and saps future growth. Difficult terms can also sometimes be imposed by aggressive lenders or investors when a business becomes less creditworthy, which can hurt a business in other ways. For instance, high late fees or the lender's ability to quickly seize important collateral can be costly and disruptive to business operations.

Cash crunch. Many companies have failed when the business runs out of cash, especially in periods of rapid growth—a problem known as "running out of runway." Owners of growth companies must make sure to manage their capital reserves carefully and be judicious in their spending. Though this last challenge may seem contradictory after the previous two, it emphasizes the need for balance. In the fighter, owners must juggle cash needs, lifestyle desires, and the true cost of their leverage. (I will share ideas on how to better manage these often conflicting issues later in this chapter.)

The Hybrid

Some hybrid models are a combination of the other two types of businesses. If you own a business like this, it is important to know your company's drivers during the different stages of the business cycle. This allows for optimal planning. A strong hybrid has healthy cash flow and is also scalable, allowing for a competitive exit value. This would be the best of both worlds: plenty of free cash flow with scalability that allows for rapid growth. Some tech service businesses such as software subscription plans are examples of strong hybrids.

A weak hybrid, meanwhile, would have thin margins and limited scalability, reducing its potential exit value. A great example is, ironically, aviation. While it is possible to have an aviation-related business with high excess cash flow and exit price, it is far more common for the opposite to be true. When I was a young entrepreneurial flight instructor in Indianapolis, I heard about an opportunity to purchase the business operations of a fixed base operator (FBO—the industry term for the business operating on an airport) north of the city. After putting together investors and a management team, I quickly realized that it is very difficult to make a profit with these businesses—especially as a small standalone operation. Margins on FBOs are narrow, and we ultimately decided against purchasing this one. (A few months later I was flying for a wealth manager while learning his business.)

It's difficult to characterize a hybrid, so consider what aspects of growth, income, and cash need best describe your specific business. The most important thing to determine is the likely range of exit values so you know how it will fit into your BHBO financial plan. Over-estimating this value can have catastrophic consequences, so it's key for owners of these businesses to study the exits of similar businesses and set proper expectations as you plan. If your anticipated exit value is modest, you will need to build wealth from excess cash flows.

Family Businesses

Even though they have their unique issues and characteristics, family businesses can easily be fighter, cargo, or hybrid. According to US Census, family businesses make up nearly 90 percent of all closely held entities in the United States. A family business, according to the Census Bureau, is defined as a company in which more than one family member works or that is under family control. For purposes of this book, dynamics for family businesses mostly apply to those with multiple family members as employees or owners, which still clearly represent a high percentage of closely held businesses. The main characteristics of a family business are as follows:

Several family members work in the business. This wouldn't necessarily apply if a child under the age of 18 is working within the business or if a family member works part-time with little to no intention of building a career with the company.

There is potential intent to transition management to one or more family members. Family business transitions are one of the tax code's most complex areas, providing owners with both opportunities and pitfalls. I will discuss many of these in upcoming chapters.

There is potential intent to gift the value of the business to one or more family members. This is different from intent to transition. Sometimes owners hope to share value but not control of the business. Such intent can bring about family dynamics that should be managed in addition to knowing the ramifications of gifting when it comes to taxes, valuation, and succession.

Family businesses carry with them unique challenges, primarily that family and business goals often become closely intertwined. This is especially relevant for the BHBO who could face conflicts when trying to balance helping their family versus helping their business. Here are a few ways those potential challenges can become issues for the BHBO:

Family dynamics interfering with business decisions. When all wealth is built within a family business, it can easily create many inefficiencies. Many a TV show has sensationally highlighted the drama surrounding some of these issues, like HBO's series *Succession*, Fox's *Arrested Development*, CBS's *Dallas,* or even some episodes of CNBC's *The Profit* (I'm a huge fan). Family members outside of the business feel left out; family employees are given tasks that exceed their abilities; valuable non-family employees are jealous of perceived or actual favoritism—the list of family business pitfalls is endless.

Tax consequences. IRS rules targeting family businesses can be confusing. For instance, you would think a normal stock gift to family members is a wonderful way to incentivize and reward them to continue in the company, participate in profits, and perhaps eventually gain control. However, IRS rules closely scrutinize the value of such gifts (or succession plans), easily penalizing a seemingly tax-free gift into one that is taxable.

Exit problems. Potential buyers are wary of family dynamics and how they might impact a company's valuation. Having family members within the business can be wonderful. However, a potential buyer may not view the value of your family member in the same light as you. Buyers are wary that remaining family members may not agree with new ways of doing business, which could become problematic if the family member is in a key position. (Some resources to address these issues will be discussed in chapter 7.)

Working Capital: The Fuel That Propels Your Business Forward

I have mentioned cash a lot. Every company needs working capital, and even thriving businesses can require extra cash to grow. This is true for all three types of businesses outlined in this chapter. No matter what type of plane you're flying, if you run out of fuel, you'd better find a place to land fast, or else you're going to crash.

Where are the best sources of capital as you grow a business? Which ones are more appropriate for a cargo plane, and which are best for a fighter jet? It's key that there is alignment here. The wrong type of funding matched with the wrong type of plane is like putting the wrong type of fuel in the plane's tank. It's going to lead to malfunctions—and sometimes those can be catastrophic. As we explore sources of capital, keep in mind the type of business you are running.

There is always a cost to taking money from someone else. Always. Period. No exceptions. The key is to determine whether that cost is worth paying and the risk is worth taking. You need to fully understand the potential benefits of that tradeoff for your particular business. The cost of capital generally comes in four basic forms regardless of whether the capital is from borrowing (loans) or an investment (equity): interest rate, collateral secured, capital position to secure, and amount of control lost:

Interest rate. This is the easiest to understand: The higher the interest rate, the worse it is for the business owner. That being said, sometimes sources of capital can make this more complicated. For instance: Is the interest rate fixed or variable? Simple or compounded? Convertible (to stock) or not? A good financial advisor can help you compare apples to apples.

Collateral secured. This is also intuitive: The more collateral needed to acquire the capital, the worse it is for the owner. However, collateral usually lowers rates. For instance, credit cards are typically issued without collateral, and their interest rates are very high. Many owners start a business by allowing a capital source to attach their personal assets, such as a house or bank accounts, to the loan. However, a goal should always eventually be that glorious word *non-recourse*. This means the bank can only pursue the secured collateral, not other sources of repayment. It takes much time and building of credit history to earn this from lenders.

Capital position. When things go wrong, there is always a line of people looking to get their money back. Capital position represents their place in line. The higher their place in line, the lower the interest rate or other cost of the capital typically is. For instance, in the event of insolvency, a bank loan would take priority over the investor who received preferred stock (stock that receives a regular income payment), who would take priority over the common stock investor.

Control. This is simply the influence you give others over the control of your business and is, by far, the most difficult cost to quantify. Know that every single investment made into your business results in some loss of control, and simply be wary as to whether this cost is acceptable. For instance, the loan from Aunt Martha at 0 percent interest? Your cost could be the constant badgering at family gatherings. The minority-preferred interest to a private equity firm? This could require you to submit a slew of weekly reports. Here, again, make sure you discuss the likely true cost of capital with your team before accepting. You obviously want to access capital with the lowest overall cost.

Sources of Capital

I have listed sources of capital by my perception of which is the lowest cost to the highest cost. Growth businesses are more likely than income businesses to move further down on the list, but it is certainly wise for every business to exhaust resources from the top of the list before moving down. It's also useful to note that this same list for startup/growth financing can also be used for exits. Here are some major sources of capital:

> **Revenue.** The business uses its own revenue to fuel growth. If your business needs to grow very quickly or has big capital requirements, this might not be a viable capital solution, but it has the lowest cost and keeps you in full control of your business.

> **Your own capital**. While investing in your own business might mean lifestyle sacrifices for you and your family, it can have big benefits. Entrepreneurs are risk-takers—funding with your own capital shows yourself and others a level of commitment and is the most common way to start a business. Of course, you also maintain full control and don't owe anyone anything. It can be a great place to be.

> **Friends and family round.** The cost for this type of capital does have the potential to be very high, especially if your business doesn't succeed! Regardless, you may be able to obtain favorable interest rates and control by borrowing/providing minimal equity from this capital source. Just be certain to

memorialize all agreements in writing and try to be an honest judge of the true cost of this capital.

Small Business Administration (SBA) loan. This special type of bank loan provides favorable terms for entrepreneurs. This type of capital is well worth considering and easy to research at www.sba.gov. Some SBA loans require personal collateral; others do not. These loans are found through SBA-approved bank lenders, though sometimes the different programs can be tricky to understand. For instance, during 2020, CARES Act loans and EIDL loans, both administered by the SBA, were instrumental in helping many businesses survive the pandemic. Widely publicized were the difficulties many small businesses had in accessing these inexpensive sources of capital, especially if they did not have a relationship with a banker. It's best to be prepared with a banking relationship even before you need a loan.

Traditional bank loan. This is a bank business loan using business or personal collateral such as assets and income. The cost for this type of capital is the interest you must pay on the loan and the risk of losing your collateral if you can't pay off the loan on time. It is common to personally guarantee a business loan (with your personal balance sheet, not that of the business). This is one of the most common sources of funding, as it is relatively inexpensive, and a good banker can act as an additional intellectual resource for your business.

Government resources. Most states have many economic incentives for small businesses through tax incentives or outright financial grants. Each of these incentives will have a cost (typically a set of restrictions associated with the incentive), but usually, the terms are favorable, as the intent is for businesses to grow and provide jobs for their communities.

Capital sources in this category include direct grant programs or subsidized "accelerators"; these provide office space, mentoring, training, introductions, and other services in addition to modest amounts of capital. Ask your accountant or financial advisor about options in your area.

Nonprofit resources. Many regions have nonprofits founded or supported by successful entrepreneurs to support their business ecosystem, either through the accelerator concept or sometimes via "tech transfer" offices through local universities. While tech transfer offices primarily support academic research of students and faculty members at their respective universities, sometimes they partner with alumni or local entrepreneurs when there is a tie to the school. The best resources for finding these in your area are likely your accountant or financial advisor.

AR financing. AR financing is a loan against accounts receivable. These can be more aggressive with higher interest rates, but also more flexible in the terms of availability and speed of financing. These are usually used when short-term loans are needed, and other avenues are more difficult to obtain.

Mezzanine/debt. "Mezzanine" is the term the private equity world uses for loans given by institutions without a banking charter. Since normal banking rules do not apply, terms are more flexible but usually have a higher interest rate.

Credit cards. Technically, this is a source of bank financing, but one that typically comes at a high interest rate charge, as it requires no collateral. Credit cards can be a very useful tool for building credit, and many cards offer rewards points for paying off balances regularly. These points can add up to meaningful cost savings—*if* you have the discipline to pay off your balance every month. Otherwise, the high compounded interest rates of credit cards can be a drain on business capital.

Equity sale. The type of equity sale (common, preferred, etc.) is beyond the scope of this book, other than stating that selling part of your stock to outside shareholders can be a useful strategy, especially if the purchaser can bring you strategic help. Such help may include mentorship, connections, other sources of capital, or strategic partnerships. Many regions offer conferences where entrepreneurs can mingle, learn, and pitch to investors. Ranges of capital that can be raised at these events vary dramatically depending on the focus of the event, but the networking and learning opportunities from such events are incredibly useful for most entrepreneurs. A search for "business pitch" with your region will likely uncover opportunities. South by Southwest (SXSW), Florida Venture Forum, and DIG South are all conferences that connect businesses with investors. Some types of equity investors include the following:

- **High–net worth individuals**. These are much more difficult to find, as they purposefully stay anonymous, but they can be valuable partners if they find you or if you manage to arrange an introduction. Terms will vary greatly with each individual or office.
- **Portfolio builders**. Rather than purchase privately held companies with an intent to sell, portfolio builders look to hold a portfolio of privately held companies to provide a competitive yield for their investors. They're more likely to purchase an income (cargo) type of business.
- **Venture capital**. VC is simply a term for loans given to or equity purchased from entrepreneurs by different institutional organizations. The following is a summary of this complicated landscape, usually

tapped only by the growth- (fighter jet) type company. One useful resource for exploring this world is www. pitchbook.com.

- ○ **Angel investors**: Groups of high–net worth investors who pool money to invest in a start-up or early-stage companies
- ○ **Venture funds**: Sources of capital with defined objectives that vary based on the expertise of the organization (the type of industry, type of financing, and size of deal)
- ○ **Private equity**: Firms that look to purchase privately held companies, usually with the intent of selling at a higher price later
- ○ **Crowdfunding**: A relatively new area enabled by legislation in 2016 that allows small investors to aggregate funds into the purchase of small business stock. Because it is a new area, be careful to read the terms, as they will vary dramatically, and do your research.
- • **Public sale of shares**: Allows private companies to sell debt or equity to the public. Certainly, reserved for larger deals, selling shares of stock requires a great deal of professional assistance to navigate the legal and financial requirements.

A good business can almost always find money, but what investors and bankers believe is good and what an entrepreneur believes is good might be two dramatically different things! One common thread is always free cash flow; if you can generate that for your business, you will always be able to find sources of capital (if you even need to do so). Be very wary if your idea doesn't have a path to free cash flow, as investors/bankers will be even warier.

If you're an early-stage company and don't have free cash flow, there are options for accessing capital. Many books are written on what investors might deem good: usually evaluating your people, process, IP, target market, potential competitors, and other factors. Even more important will be for you to understand the objectives of the funder hearing your pitch; otherwise, you will be wasting everyone's time and hurting your reputation in the venture community. There is, of course, a fine line between perseverance and insanity that many an entrepreneur has had to navigate. Know the limits of what you are willing to do and how far you will go before stepping over that line. I have created a list of potential funding sources in the state of South Carolina that you can access on my website.

Designing Your Custom Aircraft: Aligning Your True North with Corporate Mission

Regardless of whether you have a fighter jet, a cargo plane, or a hybrid, as a business owner, you can align nearly every aspect of your business with your values and goals. While most of this book discusses helping you achieve personal goals for yourself and the people and causes most important to you, many universities and business programs have developed a growing list of resources for businesses seeking to create a benevolent corporate culture.

Indeed, as I write this book during the pandemic of 2020, the trust in institutions (businesses, governments, NGOs, media) has never been lower. Before the outbreak, the global public relations firm Edelman published its *2020 Edelman Trust Barometer* (https:/www. edelman.com/trust-barometer), which provides a fascinating read on this erosion of trust as measured by competence and integrity. It offers reasons and some opportunities to rebuild. As businesses ranked highest on the competence scale among institutions (versus others, like government entities), 75 percent of respondents believed businesses could be a force for good in society. Couple that with 64 percent who say they want to buy products from companies reflecting their values and 73 percent who want to be able to say that their work changes society, and it is easy to see that the opportunity to rebuild trust through the business of the BHBO is tremendous.

As a business owner, you must keep corporate profitability and liquidity paramount; otherwise, all your noble goals can't be achieved. However, businesses that successfully balance profitability with some of these more sustainable corporate goals may better align with the founder's mission and possibly reap rewards from a grateful community. In other words, you can make payroll *and* make a difference. This, too, can impact the way you design your business and create your corporate structure.

A heartfelt and deliberate corporate mission statement can be a great start. Many an owner has gone through the actions of hiring a consultant or creating a corporate mission statement for themselves. Here, again, it can be very useful to reference your personal compass so that both your personal and corporate mission statements are aligned with your true north. Many examples abound with a quick internet search.

Another great read, *Intentional Integrity: How Smart Companies Can Lead an Ethical Revolution*, by former Airbnb Chief Ethics Counsel Robert Chesnut, discusses integrity as a corporate "superpower," the void it can fill, the ways a leader can promote it throughout their business, and the benefits it can create for customers, employees, shareholders, and society.

As these areas are somewhat new in management literature, they carry different definitions depending on the author, but ESG (environmental, social, and governance) impact (local and international), corporate citizenship, inclusive stake holding, triple bottom line, and corporate responsibility are all terms common to these relatively new movements. Researching and including some of these concepts into your business may be a way to align it with your true north.

Employee engagement. 2021 was infamous for "The Great Resignation"—very low unemployment and difficulty in attracting and retaining employees, a major concern of most businesses. It's no secret that happy employees stay and are usually more productive. What are tools for employee engagement for the BHBO? A 2021 Pew Research Center study found the top reasons for employees leaving were: pay too low, limited advancement opportunities, child-care issues, limited work hour flexibility, and uncompetitive benefits. Deloitte also conducted a 2021 survey that found Millennials, who are currently one-third of workforce but expected to comprise up to 75% of workforce by 2025, choose to work for an organization that aligns with their values. Since this is a massively broad topic, I have included some useful resources on my website for a broader discussion but following are some important starting points. First, coordinating with your benefits consulting team to make sure you have a competitive package for your market can address some of the concerns in the Pew study. They can help you compare what you are doing to your peers and make specific benefit recommendations (some of which I cover in Chapter 7). Another area that has been around for decades but is finding renewed interest is considering forms of employee ownership. I discuss ESOP's in some detail in Chapter 8, but ESOPs are only one of many forms of ownership you could potentially share in the company. Some of these forms of ownership, like stock appreciation rights or phantom stock, don't actually involve stock ownership or voting rights—they simply give employees a stake in the future success of the company. When coupled with a communication program that shares how employee's productivity can directly lead to increases in company value, studies have shown real productivity increases, not to mention the sense of pride and purpose you could foster within your workforce. The National Center for Employee Ownership www.nceo.org is a great resource in these areas.

Environmental, social, and governance (ESG). Used primarily in the context of an investment screen for companies meeting one or more of these criteria. Environmental is environmentally friendly (subject to varying standards), social can be both treatment of employees and/or position on certain social issues like LGBT or minority rights, and governance is voting structure and oversight of management—primarily to promote long-term versus short-term decisions.

Corporate citizenship/social responsibility. Frequently companies will have departments dedicated to one or more of these issues under this name. They also frequently promote corporate campaigns around charitable giving.

Triple bottom line. Definitions vary, but in general, this is an approach to business that endeavors to show that profits are not the only bottom line of a business. In addition to profits, success may be measured by impacts on and benefit to society, the environment, or people, factors companies may or may not try to quantify. Triple bottom line has been a topic of much conversation in academic journals such as *Harvard Business Review*. It can be executed by inclusion within corporate documents or mission statements.

Sustainability. Has been used in a similar context as triple bottom line, though I've seen it focused more on environmental issues. Sustainable implies that business activities can continue in perpetuity without harming important surrounding resources (people, environment).

Benefit corporation. A new form of for-profit business entity in some states requires businesses to consider society, employees, and the community in their corporate governance. A benefit corporation includes these considerations in addition to profits as part of official corporate decision-making.

Certified B corporation. This is a new type of company that voluntarily meets the highest standards of social and environmental performance. B Lab is a nonprofit that certifies these types of businesses, which must meet a rigorous checklist of social, governance, and environmental standards (bcorporation.net). Formed in 2008, B Lab has certified more than 1,600 companies within the United States, according to its website.

Know Your Airplane

You may be pleased to know that even though many skills are transferable from one aircraft to the next, every pilot receives extensive training specific to their aircraft before they are allowed to fly it by themselves. A fighter ace cannot hop into a cargo aircraft and safely fly without training. Each aircraft has its own systems, its own checklists, its own flying characteristics that must be learned to be able to safely reach its destination.

The same holds true for your business. Business schools do talk about growth versus income (fighter versus cargo), they talk about raising funds, they talk about how to make the business successful, with thousands of examples of success or failure. Even so, hardly any of them discuss what the business can do for the business owner—especially the BHBO who has unique goals. And, most business owners did not even attend a business school, leaving these areas little understood among the people doing so much of the work. Make sure you understand the type of business you are running so you can understand how it can best help you reach your destination while remaining aligned with your compass.

Chapter 6

When Things Go Wrong: Emergency Checklists and Parachutes

▬ ▬ ▬ ▬ ▬ ▬ ▬ ▬ ▬ ▬

"MOST GREAT PEOPLE HAVE ATTAINED THEIR GREATEST SUCCESS
JUST ONE STEP BEYOND THEIR GREATEST FAILURE."
–NAPOLEON HILL

Most pilots spend their entire careers without experiencing engine failure. Still, all pilots are required to memorize and practice emergency procedures, including for engine failures. Disaster preparation is always an aviator's focus, even before takeoff. What will I do if things go wrong? This is always on our minds.

More than twenty years ago, while flying a Cessna with a dear friend near Indianapolis, I faced a rare test of my emergency training. Right after takeoff, as the plane was still ascending, the plane's engine died. I can still remember every detail clearly as if it happened yesterday. Time moved in slow motion. I became hyper-focused on my emergency checklist. As my friend sat terrified only a few inches away, I raced through the items on the list: oil pressure, fuel flow, magnetos, carb heat, calling mayday. Happily, I spotted a small field next to a women's prison and was able to glide over the trees and bring the plane down safely—no injuries or damage. I was well trained, well prepared, and skilled enough to avoid disaster. I'll never forget the prison security guards coming over to see what we were doing there. You can only imagine what they were thinking!

Regardless of the type of business you run, preparing for emergencies can make a big difference in your ability to navigate a safe landing. Just like a prepared pilot, financial planners help business owners focus on emergency contingency plans *before* executing tactical or investment strategies. They want you to be prepared in the event of death, disability, disaster, or a business cash crunch. They want you, your family, and your business to stay safe, no matter what curve balls life throws your way. This chapter is for the BHBO who wants to be prepared. I'll show you how to create and use emergency checklists and parachutes to help you navigate life's storms and land safely back on terra firma.

Emergencies Related to Our Fragility

Every business owner hopes to have a long, healthy life and pass away peacefully at the ripe age of 100-plus. Unfortunately, none of us knows what the future holds. As I have mentioned several times, if you do not have an estate plan, the government has one for you. Unfortunately, the government's plan will not take care of the people you love or manage the assets you've built in the way you intended. For business owners, especially owners with children, having an estate plan in place is critical. Consider just a few of the following horrific scenarios:

> **Catastrophic taxation.** Without significant planning, an unexpected death can lead to potentially catastrophic taxation. Federal and state taxes can reach 52 percent of an estate,

forcing the sale of assets at a loss to pay a massive tax due within a year after death. As I mentioned earlier in the book, this type of taxation has decimated many families—not just from the tax itself but also from being forced to sell illiquid assets to pay the taxes. This can further crater the remaining value of those assets for the survivors. Happily, in 2022, estates valued at less than $12,060,000 for single or $24,120,000 for married couples will pay no federal tax, which excludes most estates. This estate tax has changed dramatically through the years: applying to estates as little as $675,000 back in 2001 to being eliminated for a year in 2010, to reaching top rates of nearly 80 percent in the 1970s to 40 percent today (the 52% referenced earlier included state estate taxes). Keeping plans up to date based on the latest tax code is critical. In my experience, catastrophic taxation destroys primarily those who took no action to plan for the inevitable taxes on their estate. Intelligent planning can almost always dramatically reduce the negative impacts of estate taxes.

Minor children assigned to the wrong guardians. Absent guardians named for minor children (the definition of minor depends on your state), the courts will decide through a probate process who will take care of your children in the tragic event that both parents die. If you've ever been to any court process, you realize the utter crapshoot this becomes as probate courts are notoriously overwhelmed and understaffed. The worst case is the courts cannot find a relative it believes is suitable to take care of your children, and it assigns your child to the Department of Social Services. To avoid such a horrific outcome, you must legally name guardians for all of your minor children.

State intestacy laws are arbitrary. Every state has its own laws of intestacy, which dictate how the courts will treat your estate in the absence of a will. These laws designate who is entitled to what and how much. These laws rarely match the wishes of the BHBO. For instance, some states give 50 percent to children and 50 percent to the surviving spouse. But what if the grandparents have already provided for the grandchildren? Would more be better for the spouse? In other states, the spouse gets 100 percent of the estate. What if it's a second marriage and there is some friction between your children and your current spouse? It's very unlikely these default rules are right for your family.

Minors cannot use financial assets by themselves. While the laws of legal adulthood are different in many states, a minor is not allowed to control assets that they received, even if those assets were intended for their benefit. This means that someone else (a named guardian, personal representative, or trustee) must decide when and how the assets are to be used. The problem with this approach is obvious: Expenses such as tuition, food, and housing may be left unpaid as the courts try to figure out who will be responsible for these decisions. The most common items I see that can become trapped until the children come of age are life insurance and retirement plan proceeds with minors as beneficiaries. It can be avoided by naming guardians or trustees.

Many states don't accept copies of wills. It would stink to have an elaborate estate plan that isn't even honored. Most states require original, signed estate planning documents to avoid a lengthier proving (or probate) process. Make sure you keep originally signed documents in a safe place that your loved ones can find; the courts may not accept copies.

Corporate or individual trustee chooses not to accept responsibility for trust. Imagine you spend hours putting together a perfect plan, then the trustee, after months of deliberation, decides not to accept responsibilities. Unfortunately, this means the assets can be frozen for extended lengths of time, creating even more uncertainty right at the time of most financial need—after a loved one passes away. This can be especially difficult if all assets are held in a trust. A good practice is to leave at least some liquid assets to the beneficiary directly.

Unexpected disability. If you have no legal documents, none of your assets can be managed while you're unconscious or otherwise mentally disabled. This means assets held in your name become frozen, business decisions are not made, contracts cannot be signed, and your financial world enters limbo until your recovery. A power of attorney can maintain continuity.

The Checklists You Need to Avoid Calamity

Effective estate plans can be quite simple or elaborate, depending on the size of your estate and the objectives you have as a BHBO. I have seen high-value estates effectively managed with a simple plan; most of these cases don't include children that need care, so most of the estate goes to charity. Similarly, I've seen small estates that require elaborate plans for children with special needs, multiple marriages with children, and other complex scenarios. The most important part of an estate plan is simply to have one—even if it's simple at first.

Estate planning is easy to avoid for those of us who tend to procrastinate. The concept of your own mortality is uncomfortable to consider and hopefully won't happen anytime soon, so it seems as if you can always get to it later. That is, until one day it's too late. We have precious little control over when we expire, as God, fate, or chance ultimately decides the timing of our last breath. The BHBO is almost always known for the courage it takes to make hard decisions, and the implementation of these plans is essential to remaining aligned with your true north. The process of estate planning is closely related to Covey's first principle (mentioned in chapter 1): "beginning with the end in mind." When faced with our own mortality, the trivial distractions of our lives fall away in favor of the most important things. Estate planning is not just crunching numbers and minimizing taxes: It is more essentially providing for those very people and causes most important to you.

Thus, the best way to start estate planning isn't by compiling your balance sheet and counting your pennies. The best way for the BHBO to start planning is by imagining who and what will most need your help if you're no longer around. Then you can decide what type of help they'll need, understanding that help isn't always in the form of money.

To begin, ask yourself these questions:

- Who are the people most important to me?
- What type of help would they need if I weren't around?
- Whom would I want to care for my minor children?
- Do my important people have special considerations, like special needs, management of health issues, or specific goals that I would like to assist with?
- Who has the financial acumen to manage my financial affairs?
- Do I need an objective third party like a trustee to manage any potential conflicts between my important people?
- Do I plan to support charitable causes? Do I hope these gifts are one-time, ongoing, or potentially tied to certain activities I support? Should my important people be involved in these decisions?
- Will my business have a significant loss of income if I'm not around?
- Based on the last question, what is the best disposition of the business if I'm not around: planned liquidation, sale, or continuation with key people?
- If I'm disabled, who do I trust to manage my personal and business affairs while I recover?

Only after answering these questions can you start talking with your advisory team—as discussed in chapter 3—about the type of documents needed to meet your goals.

Several key documents can help you implement your plan. I am hopeful this list arms you with enough information to go to your team with a basic understanding of estate planning.

Personal Documents

Following is a list of important personal documents your team can help you establish.

Family love letter or ethical will. This is a few paragraphs or a letter you can write as part of estate documents that have no real legal authority but that help to share the values, stories, and sentiments that you want to be shared with your loved ones as comfort or wisdom during a time of loss. People call them different things, and there is no standard industry name. Services such as Everplans and Greenbox allow you to create a family love letter, organize your vital documents, and save important digital information such as passwords; these are then released only on proof of your demise. While many movies have dramatized a video or letter embedded with some shocking truth, in reality, these are simple, heartfelt goodbyes. To create your family love letter, an easy way to get ideas flowing is by sharing important stories, and then tying them to expressions of love, wisdom through stories, or hopes for your loved ones' future. You might like what you wrote so much that you share it while alive—nothing wrong with that!

Last will and testament. Frequently a short document, the will is the foundational document of any estate plan. It outlines how your assets will be distributed and managed at the time of your death; it also names important people who will handle your affairs and take care of your survivors. This one document helps you avoid many of the thunderstorms discussed earlier—and it is critical if you have minor children.

Appointment of a guardian for minor children. This is not a separate document—it can be as short as one paragraph within a will—but of all the legal documents, this is the most important part. Without it, the selection of guardians will be out of your control after your passing. It's also an important first step in estate planning, as the choice is truly difficult: *Who will raise my children if my spouse and I are no longer alive?* It is most important to choose someone with values consistent with yours and gain a commitment from them, with the understanding that your documents will provide financial support.

Living trust. Living trusts are established while you are alive to hold assets and help designate what happens to these assets after a death or disability. Frequently a will sends most assets not already owned by the trust into it (this is called a pour-over will). The reason these are useful is that assets titled in these trusts avoid probate and can be transferred without the courts. This saves probate fees and, more importantly, allows your trustee to move assets to your beneficiaries more quickly. It's common for bank accounts, cars, investment accounts, and real estate to be held in these trusts. Even better, because they're "living," you are the trustee while alive, having full control to move assets into or out of the trust without a tax consequence. Many of the following techniques can be embedded into the living trust, making it usually a much longer, more sophisticated document. Just a quick note: Beneficiary designations like those on retirement accounts or life insurance policies also transfer directly to the beneficiaries with no probate. Avoiding probate either through a living trust or with a beneficiary designation can greatly simplify what happens after you pass.

QTIP (qualified terminal interest property). This is a silly acronym, but an effective vehicle for making sure your assets reach your children and grandchildren after you pass while taking care of your spouse. It protects the assets from potential creditors and restricts them from access by your spouse's future romantic partners ahead of your children. This trust is usually testamentary, meaning it is written within your estate documents but activates at death. It gives your surviving spouse access to income and some ability to withdraw from the principal to maintain their current lifestyle, but these assets must go to your chosen beneficiaries when your spouse passes. (A client once joked that he wanted to make sure his daughters received his assets and not the "guy with the gold chain.") Of course, the wife didn't want the "bleach blonde" to take the assets either!

Trusts. A trust is a legal entity that you create to manage assets on your behalf for beneficiaries you choose. In the hands of a good tax and estate attorney, a well-designed trust can achieve a long list of objectives: reducing exposure to estate taxes, reducing the risk of losing assets from lawsuits, and providing for the unique needs of your family and other beneficiaries. While the most important part of your role is deciding how you want to take care of your family or charities so your team can implement, it can still be very helpful to know some of the lingo. Following are a few terms and their meaning as they relate to trusts.

- **Irrevocable/revocable:** This type of trust dictates whether assets placed into the trust can be removed or controlled easily. Irrevocable trusts are usually designed to protect assets and require the grantor to give up most control over the gift. A revocable trust can be changed anytime, providing full control but no protection of assets.

- **Testamentary:** This just means "at death," so a testamentary irrevocable trust is written within estate documents but activates at death, where the trustee, not the beneficiaries, is going to be responsible for following the guidelines of the trust.
- **Grantor:** This is the person(s) funding a trust.
- **Trustee:** This is the person(s) in control of the trust. The trustee decides how to manage the assets within the trust and how and when to distribute assets to beneficiaries consistent with your wishes within the document. The choice of a trustee is another very important decision you will make, and the trustee can be an individual or corporation. While alive, unless you're looking to make a gift or protect assets from liability, you are usually the trustee. Corporate trustees are chosen when you do not know a person with the financial acumen or objective disposition to act as trustee. Sometimes a corporate trustee is named as a co-trustee to help make financial decisions for an individual trustee with less financial acumen.
- **Beneficiary:** This is the person(s) receiving benefits from the trust.
- **Ascertainable standard:** Not quite as complicated as it sounds on the surface, this essentially means what is needed to maintain one's lifestyle. It generally includes costs of health, education, maintenance, and support.
- **Special needs trust:** For families with special needs children, this trust can be a lifeline for your child. Written by attorneys who specialize in this area,

these trusts intend to safeguard assets such as financial assets or real estate for as long as they're alive. These trusts still allow a child to be eligible for some government-provided benefits.

Documents for Disability

The chances of being disabled are far higher than they are that you will pass early, yet the financial consequences can be far more devastating for the unprepared. A disability not only robs your ability to conduct normal financial affairs but also carries the unknown of when a disability will end along with the added costs of health care and maintenance. Happily, a few legal documents can help those you trust continue to keep important things running while you are disabled.

Power of attorney (POA). A POA allows someone you trust (called an "attorney in fact") to manage affairs on your behalf by giving them powers to make decisions, control accounts, and execute documents. As you might expect, you have full control to designate when these powers come into effect and what decisions your attorney is allowed to make. For instance, you can grant your spouse POA only if you are disabled (this is called springing power) and only over your personal financial affairs, while you designate separate powers to a business colleague to manage your business. A living will specifies your wishes if you're on life support and the brain becomes inactive. A health care power of attorney allows a trusted family member or friend to make medical decisions on your behalf if you are unable.

Business Documents

Of course, businesses have a far different set of needs and concerns when one of its owners dies or becomes disabled. Even though some personal estate documents can help with parts of a transition (like giving stock shares to a surviving spouse who can then make decisions), usually such documents are not effective for the continuation of a business. The main document that addresses contingency plans for the business in the event of an owner's death or disability is the buy/sell agreement.

These documents arrange what will happen to your business and the shares of the business under a wide range of circumstances, including death and disability. Much like state-specific intestate rules that govern what happens if an estate has no will, each state has different rules surrounding what happens to your business if you pass. These statutes may even be different between the type of business (LLC, C corporation, S corporation, or professional Corporation). Thus, it is important to make sure you have a buy/sell agreement that works for the shareholders and their goals. These documents can be quite simple (you're the only owner and just want to liquidate the business in an orderly manner) or very complex (multiple owners with the intent to transition the business to family members). It is always good to have an idea of the business's value when starting these conversations, as it can help with coordinating personal business planning and the individual needs of survivors. Following are some of the questions you need to ask and the decisions you need to make so your team can help implement them.

- **Do you believe the business has a good chance of survival without you?** If not, an orderly plan of liquidation is probably the best option to maximize the value to your family. It can also help your survivors resist the temptation to try and continue your business (at a great loss) to honor a legacy you did not intend to or continue to pay employees with the cash you intended for your survivors.
- **Who could successfully run the business?** Include these people in documents and compensate as appropriate.

- **What resources do they need to continue the business?** This might include cash through a key life insurance policy or the hiring of other talent.
- **What is the ideal ownership scenario?**
- **Would you need to have added incentives to retain or reward the players who could continue your business?** For instance, a nonqualified deferred compensation plan that is generous but only vested if the employees remain with the company for a few years? I will discuss specific tools to assist in these efforts in the next chapter as they also lend themselves nicely to planned buyouts.

These are important questions that should be identified and answered in the documents along with the method of the transfer. It may also be appropriate to purchase life insurance to fund the buy/sell along with key insurance to provide operating capital. Once you've made these decisions, the following are some of the types of agreements your team may recommend:

> **Entity redemption:** This simply means the company will buy out the shares from departing shareholders. Several tax pitfalls await the unwary within entity redemption plans. One is that the remaining shareholders may not get a step up in basis. This can considerably increase the tax consequence on a future sale. Transactions can also be recharacterized into less favorable tax treatment with multiple tools the IRS has in its arsenal, especially for family businesses. You may think you will pay no tax or minimal tax only to be surprised by a large tax bill. Be sure to have a skilled drafting attorney help navigate these issues.

> **Cross purchase:** Shareholders will buy the interest from the departing shareholder. Cross purchase agreements can avoid many of the pitfalls of entity redemption plans, such as

increasing the tax basis for remaining shareholders. To help fund the buyout, shareholders typically own life insurance for their partners. If there are three or more partners, however, the number of policies can get unwieldy. Four stockholders would require sixteen policies as each shareholder needs a policy on each of the other shareholders. A simplified method is to create a trusteed buy/sell, which greatly reduces the number of policies while still offering the advantages of cross-purchase agreements. This type of agreement holds one policy on each shareholder and divides the proceeds appropriately to each shareholder for the subsequent purchase.

Hybrid: Hybrid agreements are written with flexibility in mind to accommodate potential future changes. A hybrid agreement gives the stockholders (cross-purchase) the ability to purchase stock from each other first. If they do not purchase after a short period, then the company is required to complete the purchase (entity redemption).

Unique Succession Concerns of the Family Business

As mentioned earlier, the IRS has created many thunderstorms for the family business to navigate, all for one main reason: Parents are likely to do nice things for children and have an incentive to undervalue these gifts. For instance, an owner may be tempted to sell their business for a very low price to a family member acting as CEO of the business. The IRS is concerned that such transactions are not going to be taxed at fair market value, and thus they won't get their cut of your flesh. Most of these special rules do not apply to unrelated parties because they are likely to negotiate a price they both believe is fair. Thus, these thunderstorms are all gotchas related to most types of gifts or transfer of stock between family members. The IRS even has a code section (318-Family Attribution) that it can use to recharacterize buy/sell transactions against a family. Do not navigate these skies without help. Following are a few tax tools available for the family business:

303 Stock Redemption (C-corporation only). C-corporations are subject to the potential double taxation of dividends, where a payment to a shareholder is both taxable to them and non-deductible by the company. The vast majority of closely-held businesses try to avoid dividends at all costs. Unfortunately, the purchase of your stock by the company can easily be recharacterized as a dividend. This can be horrific when you think you're being taxed at capital gains rates (currently 15 percent long-term in 2022) and find out that your income rate is currently 37 percent! That's $220,000 in extra tax for each $1 million. Qualifying for a 303 redemption within your estate and buy/sell documents assures capital gains tax treatment.

6166 payment plans. I mentioned estate taxes are usually due within nine months of death. If your survivors need more time to pay, this payment plan allows estate taxes to be paid over time, up to 14 years, at low interest rates for small businesses. While a useful last resort, this tool can have its shortcomings: The IRS could put a lien on the business, which could prevent the sale of assets, and the ongoing value of the business will be monitored. Most advisors recommend against using this approach unless part of a sophisticated strategy.

Tools to Help Family Wealth Be a Positive Influence on Children's Growth

Will an inheritance ruin my child's desire to be a productive member of society? This is one of the most sensitive and important areas of estate planning and is not always addressed as it is more the domain of psychologists than attorneys, CPAs, and planners. However, for the BHBO, this can be an even more important part of planning than minimizing taxes. Of course, the potential solutions usually require a good deal of thought and customized drafting specific to each family and sometimes can benefit greatly through the help of a licensed therapist. Following are some ideas we have pursued with clients to help with this important topic:

Give and watch/teach while you're alive. Give your child some money or assets, watch what they do with it, and share insights where appropriate. The unspoken contract with this strategy is usually that poor decision-making may limit future gifting.

Family meetings/financial education. I have found family meetings to discuss common financial interests and/or estate planning one of the most powerful ways to convey values and help with financial education. Families can share the reasons and values behind designing estate plans. They can bring speakers or attend financial education seminars. These meetings can be limited or expansive in scope—beginning with a description of the basic estate planning intent up to designing family mission statements and decision-making meetings on family holdings.

Set up a charitable foundation or donor-advised fund. Bringing the family together to discuss charitable giving is another powerful way to convey values and provide financial education. Family members can learn to research the financial statements of nonprofits along with their mission to assist in determining which charities are most aligned with a family's values and likely to be responsible with their gifts. Additionally, a small or large amount of the total estate can fund the charity depending on the size of the estate and family goals. Donations can be made while living, or the foundation can be a beneficiary of your estate after death.

Incentive provisions within trusts. While many trusts are designed to allow a trustee to pay beneficiaries on the standard provisions of health, welfare, education, and maintenance, you can spell out provisions on how funds are dispersed anyway you see fit. Of course, while making these provisions overly restrictive can create resentment, keeping provisions consistent with your family values can help minimize or eliminate this resentment. While it is important to work with a good drafting attorney, these trusts are the least likely mechanisms for conveying values to your loved ones. Do all you can before your estate plan is implemented, hug your kids, and take comfort in knowing higher forces are more in control.

Families with Valuable Real Estate

Aside from family businesses without succession plans, no other asset causes more family discord than valuable real estate. If left to heirs without a plan, usually decisions are postponed until one of the family members needs money—then few agree on whether the property should be rented, sold, or maintained. This can leave family members not speaking to each other for years. One solution is to hold the family real estate within an LLC. A great book, *Saving the Family Cottage* by Stuart Hollander, Rose Hollander, and David Fry, shares many of the options to consider when keeping a property in the family. An LLC holding the family cottage, thoughtfully drafted by an attorney, can address many of the potential issues of a cottage held for the benefit of the next generation.

Parachutes and Insurance

Anytime an aircraft performs aerobatic maneuvers, all passengers are required to wear a parachute to protect them when all else fails. Running a business is certainly an aerobatic maneuver, and the BHBO needs some insurance to protect them, their families, and the people they care about when all else fails.

Many despise insurance. It is an expensive cost. It can be complicated to understand. Yet risk management should be an essential idea for even the most aggressive BHBO as some risks can be catastrophic to those important to you. Of course, some insurance is required by law, including workers' compensation and health insurance. For optional coverages, consider these questions when building your insurance portfolio:

- How much is the worst-case amount of loss?
- How likely is it to happen?
- How much will it cost to purchase?

Once you have your answers, balance the total risk of loss, the likelihood of a loss occurring with the cost of the insurance. If the worst amount of loss is very high with low likelihood and low cost, it's probably worth the coverage. If the amount of loss is low, it is probably best not to purchase coverage in most scenarios. If there's a high likelihood of risk of loss along with a high amount of loss, the coverage is probably too expensive, and it might be an activity to avoid. If the likelihood of loss and cost of loss are high and the cost of loss low, buy the coverage. Following are outlines of the types of coverages and insights on their use and design.

Personal Coverages

Personal insurance coverages are important tools to help transfer the risk our personal vulnerability can translate into significant financial hardships for ourselves and our families. Most know about these coverages, but since thinking about them might be unpleasant, some will delay their purchase.

Disability insurance. Statistically, you will have a much higher likelihood of being hurt or sick and unable to work for an extended period than passing away early. Most intuitively understand this risk. Being unable to work for months or years can be as devastating as your ability to produce can vanish in the face of certain conditions. If you calculate the potential lost income using annual net earnings, you can see the impact that multiples of three, five, ten, or twenty years can have. It can quickly add up to millions of dollars in lost revenue that you might otherwise have earned. This quickly grows to many millions you and your family were dependent on. That is why most financial planners consider long-term disability the most devastating risk to working-aged people. It is far more costly than losing any piece of property, even your home. It is especially crucial to get disability insurance if you have a cargo- (income) oriented business. You can insure not only your income, but the business overhead expenses. And business buyout insurance can help keep liquidity within your business if you are absent for long periods. It is also possible, especially for more mature businesses, to self-insure as your ability to take long absences increases. In general, the best type of disability coverage is that which covers *your* job and where premiums cannot go up.

Umbrella liability insurance. A relatively inexpensive form of coverage, these policies help protect against some personal lawsuits. Due to their relatively low premium, I usually suggest clients own this type of policy to protect their personal assets and put an insurance company on the hook for helping defend you in a claim.

Life insurance. There are many critically important needs to purchase life insurance for business owners: covering family as replacement income for lifestyle, covering debts or future college expenses, providing funds for business liquidity, providing funds for business buyouts, providing funds to pay taxes, helping to equalize an illiquid estate, providing funds in the event of a loss of a key person—the list is extensive and important. The reason that life insurance is so complicated and detailed is that it is the one coverage where there is absolute certainty that there will eventually be a claim. Death and taxes are both certain—but they only sell life insurance. Thus, some life insurance policies build up a cash value toward mortality, creating unique characteristics that also come with tax advantages.

All life policies are found on a continuum, from policies that cover a limited period, for a small amount of premium, no cash value, and high death benefits (term insurance) to an investment vehicle that will have high premiums, lifetime coverage, high cash value, and low death benefits (permanent insurance). The former tries to provide the most amount of coverage per premiums paid, and the latter tries to make the most use of the tax benefits afforded to life insurance policies. The higher the death benefit in relation to the premium, the lower the growth of the cash. The tax advantages were so good on life insurance policies before 1988 they passed a law (Technical Corrections Act of 1988, defined as modified endowment contracts, or MEC) to limit their use as tax shelters. Before the act, an insured person could buy a policy for an insanely low death benefit—essentially eliminating the cost of life insurance coverage and becoming a pure investment vehicle. The new law mandates a maximum level of premiums per death benefit to enjoy most of the tax benefits. Additionally, many insurance companies have designed their policies for high premium payments with very low costs, making the IRR (internal rate of return) extremely competitive.

There are two things about life insurance consumers usually don't know—variable commissions and crediting rates. Most commissions are paid on providing death benefits—if an insurance policy is designed to limit death benefits (within the constraints of the new MEC law previously discussed), the costs of coverage are much less, which allows the insurance to grow a higher cash value. Some companies offer institutional life policies (COLI or BOLI) with a limited commission and high rates of return on cash, though premiums are expected to be in the hundreds of thousands or millions. It is even possible for high–net worth individuals to design and implement their own life policies (PPLI—private placement life insurance), for the specific purpose of keeping the cost of insurance down and thus the net rate of return high. Thus, if you seek to build cash within your policy, make sure you design it such that the death benefits and/or commissions are minimized to your benefit.

Aside from some creative tax techniques using life insurance with corporations I'll discuss in the next chapter, term insurance or other forms of coverage (like universal life) that keep premiums to a minimum are the best options for most people. While permanent insurance can accomplish promoted cash value goals if held for fifteen or more years, life has too many uncertainties, making it statistically rare for people to own permanent coverage for a long time. The reasons people have canceled coverages are many: the insurance company providing a poor rate of return, new options on policies becoming more attractive for your situation, or just having a cash flow need such that it is not practical to continue coverage.

If cash flow is ample and other savings (like retirement plans or IRAs) are already utilized, then life insurance with cash value can make a lot of sense—again, as long as the time horizon is very long (ten years or more). Even though there are costs of insurance and liquidity limitations, the tax benefits can be quite like a Roth IRA: Premiums are not deductible, but cash grows tax-deferred, and cash value can usually be accessed cash free through loan provisions. Just be sure to compare using your most trusted financial calculator's IRR (internal rate of return) calculation. For instance, a well-designed policy maximizing cash can provide a market-type rate of return (8 percent or more), whereas a poorly designed policy can languish at rates of return of less than 3 percent.

In the past few years, some companies have added long-term care benefits to life insurance policies. Since long-term care is another area with a high likelihood (though not a certainty) of a claim, I have found these types of policies an interesting form of tax-favored self-insurance. Most allow continued access to cash values while providing a limited death benefit in addition to the long-term care benefit. The main benefit, in my opinion, is that growth of the premiums becomes tax-free if used for a long-term care expense—which can be more competitive than funding long-term care on your own. Just like anything, it's good to judge the pros and cons for yourself.

A simple formula for purchasing a life insurance policy is as follows:

- Determine the amount of coverage you need.
- Determine the length of time you need it (might maintain, might decrease as time goes on).
- Determine cash flow availability (compared to other options).

Once you've figured out these questions, you can design an appropriate policy.

Corporate Coverages

I encounter few experienced business owners who aren't familiar with corporate insurance coverages—partially as much coverage is required by law (workers' compensation, leveraged real estate, health insurance) and partially as the professionals who sell these coverages are quite good at explaining what is needed. Thus, I will try to provide a few insights on how these coverages can help the BHBO take care of their business and employees when these emergencies arise.

Group health. The health landscape has changed dramatically after the Affordable Care Act and will continue to change as the branches of government continue to change the rules. While this makes reliance on a health insurance specialist essential, these professionals have grown such that assistance navigating coverages have become a smaller part of the value they bring. Many will help with compliance, communication technology, assistance with human resource management, data analytics, risk control, and other consulting functions. Make sure your specialist does far more than sell you coverage. For the BHBO, health insurance is a critical benefit to your employees and worth some careful consideration to be sure your employees remain well covered and motivated. While it is impossible to predict the next change coming out of Washington, there are a few trends worth watching: as HSAs (health savings accounts) are probably the most tax-efficient vehicle on the planet, high deductible plans are rapidly gaining in popularity and adoption; COVID has accelerated the trend toward telehealth; many insurers have different types of wellness programs focusing on preventative coverage; and some larger employers implement self-insurance programs that can be cost-effective.

Casualty coverages. Casualty coverages (property, equipment, inventory, etc.) vary dramatically in cost, so it is quite important to be sure you are working with a professional familiar with your industry. It is common for insurance carriers to specialize within industries, and they can even restrict the agents/agencies who can sell their policies, further pointing to the importance of a good casualty firm.

Liability coverages. Normally, the same agency will handle both coverages, but it is important to understand the differences. Certainly, any company can be subject to a lawsuit, but each industry has unique risk profiles for the types of liabilities that can harm them. For instance, a manufacturer would have risks in association with their products, such as delivering on time or defects. Medical practice has a completely different liability in medical malpractice. Losing a lawsuit can only crater your business and perhaps personal balance sheet. It is an exhausting experience, which is why it is good to have a quality insurance company in your corner.

Workers' compensation. Perhaps no insurance has as wide a spread of premium payments for the same coverage as workers' compensation due to the complicated nature of how each employer is rated (experience modification, or MOD). Here, again, working with a professional is important—it is especially important to help implement risk management programs to keep your employees safer and your MOD low.

Making Your Own Parachute: Captive Insurance Companies

An innovative technique gaining adoption for even medium-sized companies is self-insuring through forming your own insurance company, called a "captive insurance company." If your insurance premiums exceed a couple hundred thousand dollars a year, these may be worth consideration. The tax savings and opportunities to reduce overall net premium payments are significant. The BHBO owner can also give employees or family members ownership that might reduce taxes or provide incentives.

At its core, a captive is nothing more than formalized self-insurance, either with risks manageable on their own or with a very high deductible and another insurance company insuring against the largest of claims. For instance, I've seen captives write warranty coverage as the risks were fairly predictable and limited (self-insurance). I've also seen a captive established to handle risks like general liability coverages and purchase a very high deductible policy from a "reinsurer" (an insurance company that sells coverage to other insurance companies) to avoid a catastrophic loss. Captives can cover nearly any type of risk, including casualty and health/life insurance–related risks. Captives can be established in many jurisdictions based on your objectives. My home state of South Carolina has good legislation, as do offshore locations such as Bermuda or the Cayman Islands. Who doesn't like visiting Charleston or Grand Cayman?

Any form of self-insurance carries risk since large or unexpected claims can eat up the premiums and void the hoped-for objectives mentioned. However, suppose the risk is reasonably well understood. In that case, the potential for either premium savings and/or "underwriting profits" (where premiums exceed the claims) are significant, which can be another source of supplemental wealth accumulation.

As a separate business entity with growth potential, these entities' ownership can be used creatively to benefit family members or employees. For instance, one family formed a captive within an LLC structure that gave the parents control while giving most of the value to their daughters. This allowed the growth to accumulate and pass to the next generations without estate taxes (this family saved over $3 million in estate taxes). Another family established a benefits program (discussed in the next chapter) funded with captive stock for key people: The growth of the captive provided a meaningful retirement pool of money for key people, strict vesting provisions were added to provide a strong incentive to remain, and the overall cost to the company was minimal given it was already paying the insurance premiums.

Checklists Memorized and Parachutes Packed

As is commonly experienced by those well trained in emergencies, I did not feel fear or other emotions when I had the engine failure; I was completely focused—at least until after I had landed in that field next to the prison. After confirming my passenger and I were safe and secure, the rush from what happened carried over all of us—thank goodness we are alive! The security guards walked up cautiously, their hands on their firearms; it was all we could do not to hug them. Being within the city limits of Indianapolis with over a million people, finding the field where we landed was truly a needle in a haystack. I can recall my thinking as we flew after completing the emergency checklist and calling *Mayday! OK, International is only 5 miles away. If it quits now, I can slow it down into these trees and we'll have a good chance of surviving.* I continued to assess. *That water will be too cold in March . . . That interstate is too heavily traveled. Wait! That field will work!* I quickly prepared the airplane for landing, turned into the heavy wind, and settled down into a field 1,300 feet long (most runways are at least 3,000 feet). The FAA, who interrogated me in a black Crown Victoria immediately after the incident said, "Great job. Only wish you had landed closer to the road, so my car didn't get stuck in the mud." As Louis Pasteur said, "Chance favors the prepared mind."

Having checklists prepared and parachutes packed on your journey does more than keep you and those you care about ready for things going wrong; it prepares you and your business for things going *well.* One of the most important value drivers of any business is the ability for the business to survive without you (after you sell), so this type of preparedness can lead to your business being better prepared for your eventual exit and thus a higher valuation. It also helps initiate ideas and priorities for living the rewarding life and lifestyle of a BHBO as you take care of your people, as I will discuss in the next chapter.

CHAPTER 7

Enjoying the Flight: Tools for the Journey

— — — — — — — — —

"I HAVE WANDERED ALL MY LIFE, AND I HAVE ALSO TRAVELED; THE
DIFFERENCE BETWEEN THE TWO BEING THIS, THAT WE WANDER
FOR DISTRACTION, BUT WE TRAVEL FOR FULFILLMENT."
—HILAIRE BELLOC

If you have been following the steps in this book, you have taken the time to understand your true north as a BHBO. You have written your mission statement as your compass. You have built your advisory team as your air traffic controllers. You have put in place tools to implement your vision and monitor your progress. You have a clear understanding of the type of business you're "flying," and have put in place a contingency plan to protect your business, your employees, your loved ones, and your BHBO goals. Congratulations, you're building a strong foundation for your future! Now it's time to start enjoying the journey.

Running a business is challenging on so many levels. Fulfillment and enjoyment for the BHBO do not need to wait until completing a large exit; it can come from enjoying some of the fruits of success, building wealth for you and your family, and from the process of taking care of those people and causes that define your true north. Happily, many tools have been created that help business owners achieve their goals as even the government incentivizes people to pursue business ownership and goals typical of the BHBO, like charitable giving. In this chapter, I will try and aggregate many of these tools so you can be informed as you assess your options with your advisory team. It's going to be fun!

Every successful business eventually becomes an engine of free cash flow. The fighter may be using much of that free cash flow to finance growth. The cargo will be looking for tax-efficient ways to invest or utilize it. And, of course, the hybrid will be seeking balance. How much of the cash flow should you be using to help fund your personal goals? Here is a perfect example where the BHBO financial plan, as discussed in chapter 4, can help you determine how much of the cash flow you need for each of your objectives. Sticking to this plan will help you from underfunding or overfunding any goal (retirement, college, charitable gifting) and keep you from being overly reliant on the cash from an exit. You never want to sell when you have no other choice. Having intelligently built wealth within and outside your business and consistent with goals gives you many more options.

Retirement

Few areas in the tax code can generate more tailwinds for your flight than within retirement plans. Used properly, these can dramatically accelerate the wealth accumulation for yourself, your employees, and your family as a powerful supplement to the financial engine of your business. Not only are these powerful tools for building retirement wealth for yourself, but they can be used creatively to assist in funding buyouts, as I will discuss in the next chapter. Knowledge and use of these plans for the BHBO can easily mean the difference in millions of dollars due to the power of compounding interest in a tax-favored environment.

Warren Buffett called compounded growth the "8th wonder of the world" as the growth becomes exponential. Consider that if you start with $100,000 and earn simple interest (interest only on original investment) for 30 years of 5 percent, you will have grown your money to only $250,000. If that same interest of 5 percent is compounded (interest on the interest), you will have over $430,000, over four times your original investment, and nearly double simple interest! The interest on the interest starts small but grows exponentially through time. Compounded growth on tax-favored money is even more powerful as you are earning interest on money the government would otherwise receive, making it one of the most efficient ways to build wealth outside of the business. To show this power, consider the previous $100,000 example. If you get a deduction in the top bracket, you have around $185,000 in your account to start. This leaves you with about $800,000 after 30 years, almost double a taxable account.

In the last few years, including 2019 when a new major piece of legislation was passed (the SECURE Act), Congress has continually expanded on tax benefits for employers and employees within retirement plans. Among the improvements are the following: The number of allowable contributions continues to generally increase with nearly every passing year, the ability of employees to access funds pre-retirement has increased (like being able to repay student loans), more people are eligible (part-time workers), employers can combine their purchasing power to reduce cost and administrative burden (e.g., multiple employer plans or pooled employer plans), and they continue to increase the tax savings/credits for both employers and employees. The Setting Every Community Up for Retirement Enhancement Act of 2019 (SECURE) provides for tax credits up to $5,500 to set up new retirement plans. Even employees who have limited income can receive added tax credits for participating in these plans, providing a government match on top of any match you provide.

Qualified retirement plans. "Qualified" means the plan qualifies for certain tax benefits. Qualified retirement plans are among the most flexible, tax-advantaged, and useful tools for small business owners in taking care of themselves, their family, and their employees. This section will assume you have a basic understanding of retirement plans and focus on some intermediate to advanced concepts that can be particularly useful to the business owner.

Here's a quick review of all qualified retirement plans: At its most basic level, qualified plans simply afford tax benefits to those who invest in them. All of them help the investor avoid two out of three levels of taxation: contribution, growth, and distribution. In the traditional plan, the contribution is deductible, it grows tax-deferred, and taxes are finally paid at distribution (usually over many years). In the Roth 401k/IRA plan, the contribution is not deductible, but then it grows tax-free for the rest of your life (or even up to 10 years after you pass for beneficiaries). You can usually choose where you prefer being taxed based on your current tax bracket and where you expect tax rates/brackets to be at the time of distribution out of plan.

You have likely seen some of the types of qualified retirement plans, but I thought it would be helpful to include a quick review and perhaps an introduction to new vehicles for the BHBO.

> **IRA/Roth IRA:** Allow those who qualify with earned income to contribute a relatively limited amount, $6,000 for 2022, typically increasing annually (plus another $1,000 if over 50). While these are limited by both dollar amount and qualification restrictions, they can be used creatively as "icing on the cake."
>
> For instance, hiring your young children into the business has been a favorite technique for CPAs and financial advisors for years, as it allows kids to learn more about the business,

build a work ethic, and, of course, provides tax advantages. According to the Fair Labor Standards Act, 14 is the minimum age before they can be hired, but there are limitations on the type of work they can perform, so check with an advisor. Children have low tax brackets, so saving into a Roth can create millions for your children in retirement with little tax. Only $6,000 per year placed into a Roth from age 14 to 18 could grow to almost $2,500,000 tax-free income at age 65 if we assume 10 percent interest (10 percent is the approximate rate of return of the S&P 500 since its inception in 1926)! Of course, I am obliged to say that past performance is no guarantee of future returns and individual results vary. Remember what Buffett said about the eighth wonder of the world?

Also, even if you do not qualify (ask your tax advisor, generally based on income levels) for a deductible contribution, the rules currently allow for nondeductible contributions. While the Roth IRAs' income limits are very restrictive, currently there is no income limit on Roth conversions, which is converting a traditional IRA to a Roth. Thus, you could make a nondeductible IRA contribution and subsequently convert to a Roth to enjoy the tax benefits.

Simplified Employee Pension (SEP): If you are the only employee or have a few others and want the easiest plan to set up and maintain, this is likely your best choice. You can defer and deduct 25 percent of your income up to a limit that increases almost every year ($61,000 in 2022). Each employee must receive an identical percent of their salary contributed by the company, so it is not flexible, but it's simple! It's also a good plan for procrastinators as you can wait until tax filing (usually April 15th) of the following year to set up and fund.

SIMPLE IRA/SIMPLE 401k: Whereas a SEP only allows company contributions, both the SIMPLE IRA and SIMPLE 401k allow for some employee contributions within a boiler-plate retirement plan that requires very little administration. The business owner is required to make either a 2 percent of pay outright contribution or a match employee deferrals up to 3 percent to their IRAs. This allows for deferrals up to $14,000 (plus $3,000 over 50) in 2022. Talk to your advisors about the nuanced difference between these plans, which include such items as whether employee loans are allowed. I have found these types of plans useful as "starter" 401k plans where the business is still small, and large deferrals are not yet an objective.

Now that I've covered some of the basic types of retirement plans, the following are a little more complicated, but can help the BHBO create even more tax-favored wealth for themselves, their employees, and their family as the contribution limits are higher and the flexibility greater.

401k/profit sharing: This is the most traditional form of qualified plan, allowing all employees to defer their income and/or allowing the company to contribute to employees' accounts. While the law calls it "profit sharing," it has absolutely nothing to do with profits—it is simply the business owner deciding to contribute to employee accounts. A 401k allows employees higher deferrals than the SIMPLE IRA ($20,500 for 2022 or $27,000 if over 50), plus it allows for you to match all employee deferrals and add an extra contribution to all accounts (including yours). By themselves, they can be valuable tools for you and your employees. However, the profit-sharing portion is still limited to a percentage of salary, and your higher-paid employees or owners can be limited on their deferrals if your lower-paid workers are not participating in the plan. In other words, if your employees are not taking advantage of the 401k, your deferrals could be limited (called ADP/ACP testing). The next two optional plan characteristics could customize your plan to help meet additional funding goals.

Weighting contributions to different groups: It is possible to weight company contributions in favor of those who have been with the company longer, have higher salaries (to offset lack of Social Security coverage over a certain amount), and are closer to retirement. This is called "cross-testing," or 401(a)(4) of ERISA. These types of plans usually work well if your company has a high ratio of highly paid/owner-employees to non-highly paid. If the demographics of your company are a good fit, this has the net effect of allowing business owners to favor themselves or key people when making larger corporate contributions, as long as a certain percent is contributed to all other employees first. This almost always increases the amount for all employees while allowing significant contributions for you and your management team—all deductible. I have seen 90 percent or more of a corporate contribution going to key employees or family members using this technique. Even the non-highly paid employees receive much more in contributions than without cross-testing. The deduction has helped to fund the added benefits.

When management has limited deferrals: 401k plans have many tests in order to qualify for favorable tax treatment, but one of the most common is ADP/ACP testing. This test essentially limits salary deferrals of "highly compensated employees" if the "non-highly compensated employees" defer a small percent of their salaries. However, there are four separate plan options (called "safe harbors") that can exempt the plan from this test and allow highly compensated employees to defer up to the maximum. Owners can choose the safe harbor that is best for their situation. Here's where it gets fun for a nerd like me: Combining the safe harbor with cross-testing can help some owners defer up to $61,000 or $67,500 if over 50 per year—it works exceptionally well when the amount you saved in taxes exceeds the amount that you contribute to employees. Wouldn't you rather give money you'd otherwise pay in taxes to your employees?

Defined benefit (DB) plans: What if you have the ability and interest to defer more than $67,500? A defined benefit plan could do exactly that. Where a 401k is technically considered a defined contribution (meaning the contribution amount is known), a DB plan defines the dollar amount or income amount needed at retirement and then calculates the amount of contribution required to meet this goal. This is more complicated and has additional limitations versus defined contribution plans, such as that it requires more commitment on behalf of the company to make contributions, it has higher operating costs, and it carries higher risks to the company. However, if most contributions go to owners or key people, these previously discussed risks are reduced significantly, and millions in tax-favored deductions can accumulate. You can also combine this type of plan with 401k/profit sharing for added flexibility. Again, if the tax savings exceed both the costs and contributions to employees, both you and your employees can benefit significantly.

ESOPs (Employee Stock Ownership Plan), Employee Ownership, and "Open Book Management"

ESOPs are another type of qualified retirement plan with powerful succession tax characteristics that I will discuss in more detail in chapter 8. In this section, I'll describe what they are and discuss how they can be used as tools to help increase productivity and build wealth for your employees.

An ESOP is another qualified retirement plan funded primarily with company stock and is not subject to the same investment diversification requirements. However, most of the rules applying to retirement plans also apply to an ESOP. These plans give employees a stake in the outcome and growth of a company within a tax-favored environment, though their rights are different from normal shareholders since they do not own the stock in their names. Thus, company voting rights and the right to see financial information are restricted. For instance, ESOP employees typically do not have the right to see others' salaries or vote on normal business activities. The stock does not need to be publicly traded; it just needs an annual independent stock valuation. Normally, contributions come directly from the company into their ESOP accounts, similar to a company match or profit-sharing contribution. ESOPs have been around since 1974, there are nearly 7,000 of them across the country, and they cover over 14 million participants (according to NCEO in 2016). Yet, most are unfamiliar with these invaluable tools.

According to the nonprofit National Center for Employee Ownership, companies with some form of employee ownership program coupled with educating employees outperform their peers by nearly 10 percent in revenue growth while employees have over double the average in retirement funds. As mentioned earlier, I had the pleasure of working with ESOP experts from around the country while a consultant with Palmer & Cay. One of those trips included a visit to St Louis, Missouri, to attend the annual "Gathering of Games" organized by The Great Game of Business—one of the pioneers and leading organizations on "open-book management." Its founder, Jack Stack, has a fascinating story on how he and a management group purchased the company (Springfield Remanufacturing Corporation [SRC]) from International Harvester with $100,000 cash and almost $9 million in debt (a harrowing 89-1 debt to equity ratio). After observing that floor workers (most of whom didn't have college degrees) could quote and track complicated statistics from their favorite baseball teams and players, Stack became convinced that these employees could track important financials within the business—especially if given a financial interest in these numbers. With much growth and refinement, SRC quickly paid off the debt and has grown into a large conglomerate with many subsidiaries, mostly borne from employee ideas. According to their 2018 retirement plan tax filing (form 5500), SRC employees average over $1 million in their ESOP alone. Stack has since written two books that I'd highly recommend, *The Great Game of Business* and *Stake in the Outcome*.

Open book management through "Great Games" is a fairly simple concept at its core. First, share important, simplified, and department-specific financials with employees. Then create a financial game so they can track numbers relevant to them and compete on goals. Lastly, give them a stake in the outcome so they care about winning. This stake can be through profit-sharing bonuses, nonqualified deferred compensation, or through qualified plans like ESOPs. All can be powerful productivity tools when coupled with open-book management to help grow your business as they also help build wealth for your employees, and multiple consulting organizations exist (including the Great Game of Business) to help owners implement such a strategy.

Advanced Ideas with Retirement Plans

Do you own a cargo business that is like accounting, legal, or medical, as discussed in chapter 5? Using retirement plans as shown can help the business gain use of the new QBI (qualified business income) deduction for S corporations in addition to the deduction for funding the retirement plan. While the math is quite complicated and will not apply to all situations, you would receive two deductions for one contribution. If your business is a cargo, call your CPA or financial advisor! These deductions can easily save hundreds of thousands of dollars but are well beyond the scope of this book.

Are you interested in using your retirement plan for real estate or private equity? There is currently no exclusion on investing in private real estate or private equity within most retirement plans, but there are limitations. While a complex legal topic, the main limitation is to be sure that you or your family receive no current personal benefit from either type of asset; otherwise, the IRS could consider it a distribution and hit you with an unexpected tax on that distribution, including potential penalties. For instance, you cannot buy a house within your retirement plan and then live in that house.

Private equity positions within Roth accounts can be particularly interesting: While losses cannot be used to offset other capital gains, all capital gains on the holding within the Roth become tax-free. This again can amount to thousands or even millions in savings if your investment multiplies many times your initial investment. I think it important to note that in late 2021 as Congress had been debating new legislation, putting limits on Roth accounts and prohibitions on private equity within IRA's was discussed, but as of now is not included in potential legislation. Needless to say, your team must be aware of the impact of any new legislation on your financial plans.

The BHBO and Taking Care of Employees: "Retirement Readiness"

Let's face it, most Americans are not good at saving. A retirement study by Fidelity in 2019 found that the average retirement account balance for Americans was less than $100,000, which would provide less than $4,000 per year in lifetime income. Many people live paycheck to paycheck, and many business owners place their retirement plan at the bottom of the list of items they want taking up their bandwidth. However, not only do these trends hurt American's ability to retire, but this ultimately indirectly affects all business owners' bottom line through two highly related costs: health care and productivity. If an employee does not have adequate funds to retire, they will postpone retirement, exponentially increasing health care costs for group health insurance and gradually reducing the productivity of the workforce. Thus, it is a fantastic idea to work with your retirement plan consultant to focus, track, and take easy (usually low or no-cost) steps to increase your workforce's retirement readiness. The SECURE Act of 2019 has additional provisions specifically intending to help make it easier for business owners to increase their employees' retirement readiness. For instance, it increased employees' ability to auto-enroll and auto-increase, which already were the beneficiaries of certain "safe harbors" protecting owners from liability. Just as consumers like simplicity in their shopping purchasing, the industry and regulators are trying to make it easier for business owners and employees to participate in retirement plans.

Nonqualified Deferred Compensation (NQDC)

Few tools are as versatile and exciting as NQDC, the Swiss Army knife of benefits planning. Finalized in 2007, section 409(a) was established to clarify the rules that should be followed with these plans. While "nonqualified" indicates that this benefit doesn't qualify for an initial tax deduction, it does allow for the ability to defer taxes, income-shift to lower tax brackets, or provide a meaningful benefit with minimal cash. This makes NQDC an invaluable tool for both income and growth businesses. The sky is almost the limit; consider the flexibility:

- Who can be covered? Employers can choose nearly any group of employees—executives, salespeople, office staff—as long as the group chosen is not discriminatory.
- What benefits can be provided? Employers can offer profit sharing, stock-related incentives, employee deferrals, or even benefits related to the performance of their specific department. These can help link the compensation to the corporate goals you would most like to incentivize.
- How long before benefits vest? Employers can make vesting almost as restrictive (through retirement) or liberal as they want (immediate). This can help incentivize employees to stay with the company.

While I've painted an extraordinarily broad picture, most of the NQDC plans fall into the following four categories:

Stock-related benefits: These can be crafted to allow employees chosen by you a stake in the financial outcome of the business without necessarily requiring financial outlay or giving up voting rights. Phantom stock, stock appreciation rights, restricted stock, and nonqualified stock options are examples of stock-related benefits. I'll lump qualified stock options in here as well—these types of options have added tax advantages but additional rules to qualify. These are used with great effectiveness in fighter-type businesses as you can use them without diluting shares and protecting cash.

Retention plans: Crafted in such a way as to provide extremely generous benefits to employees who stay with the company for a long time, these "top hat" plans with long vesting schedules are examples of retention plans. Top-hat plans can provide a lump sum or income stream at retirement funded by the company. They can also help the employees pay for their children's college or buy a house—the sky is the limit if the elections are made more than a year in advance! These plans can be used for either a fighter or a cargo. They're useful whenever you have key people, and retention is critically important. Additionally, as discussed in chapter 8, these can be coordinated with buy/sells to help with succession planning and your eventual exit.

Split dollar: When there is a need for life insurance on an employee either for the business (like key-man insurance) or for the employee's family, the benefits of a life insurance policy can be split between the company and the employee—hence the term "split dollar." For instance, is it more important for the business to have key person insurance on the employee or to provide insurance to the family—or both? Or is the insurance part of a buy/sell agreement? Or is the tax-favored growth of life insurance cash value to be used for a buy/sell or employee retirement? You can allocate the portions of the life insurance policy in proportion to the goals you are trying to accomplish. Here, again, these types of plans are useful for both types of businesses.

Employee salary deferral: As mentioned earlier, ERISA limits the amount anyone can defer into a 401k up to $20,500 for 2022 (plus another $6,500 'make-up contribution' if over 50, totaling $27,000). However, financial planners suggest at least 10 percent salary deferral to meet most retirement goals—meaning anyone making over $200,000 a year will not be able to save enough within their 401k. Thus, SERP (supplemental employee retirement plan) can help employees with higher income defer over the qualified limits with additional tax-deferred savings. Additionally, this can also allow the company to make contributions that match deferrals a 401k may restrict. Many record keepers exist within the NQDC space that make these types of plans look nearly identical to a traditional 401k (online access, investment vehicles, etc.).

Tax Benefits NQDC to Owners

If the business is a flow-through entity (S or LLC), the tax benefits are negligible absent the use of specialized life insurance products. However, especially with the recent 2017 tax act, owners of C corporations can gain considerable tax advantages by deferring into the 21 percent corporate tax bracket when their personal brackets are much higher. In other words, if you must pay tax on profits, paying it at 21 percent can be better than 37 percent while simultaneously creating a legal obligation of the company to pay this out when hopefully your personal bracket is lower. If qualified plans are maxed out, this can be a useful additional wealth accumulation tool.

Tax Benefits NQDC to Employees

Employees see the same tax advantages as qualified plans, making these attractive means of tax deferral.

The Fine Print

There's never something for nothing, right? The assets within non-qualified plans are subject to the claims of corporate creditors; thus, if the company files for bankruptcy, monies in the plan are at risk. The company also does not enjoy a deduction on funding these plans; they only receive a deduction when they're finally paid out to employees. Thus, it is useful to consider tax-favored funding vehicles, one of the reasons many large corporations use institutional "COLI" or corporate-owned life insurance for tax-deferred funding. However, depending on the type of design, no funding is required (don't need to fund until payout)—but it's important to have a plan to be sure cash is ready when the payout is due. It is thus sometimes common to separate assets intended for NQDC into a vehicle called a rabbi trust, which restricts the company's use of the money, though it is still subject to creditors' claims.

Wealth Building Tools That Are Not Retirement Related

Why should retirement plans have all the fun? Even though the types of plans aren't as great, the following are a few tax-favored savings ideas for funds not used for retirement.

> **529 plans:** 529 plans are also one of the most powerful and flexible tools within the tax code. They are intended to be used to pay for college and/or K–12 school expenses. Their power

comes from their tax-free growth if used for education, a state income deduction in certain states, and the ability to make a gift outside of your estate while still maintaining the ability to control and recapture the asset if the situation changes. The penalties for withdrawing out of a 529 are also modest: All principal can be recovered without penalty, and only interest will be taxed as income plus a 10 percent penalty. What many do not know is that many state plans also allow corporate 529 plans sponsored by a company. The tax benefits are identical, but the costs associated with group plans are usually lower, plus employees have the convenience of a payroll deduction.

HSA plans: Health savings account plans are savings vehicles associated with high deductible health plans, which are gaining in popularity among both individual and group health plans. Retirement plans and 529 plans help avoid two levels of taxation. HSA plans, when used for medical needs, avoid every level of taxation, which means money put in an HSA is completely tax-free! These funds are tax-deductible, grow tax-deferred, and can be used tax-free. To my knowledge, it is the only vehicle avoiding every level of US income taxation and one reason contributions are strictly limited. If you have a high-deductible health insurance plan, do not miss on funding these vehicles!

Real estate: Real estate with a business or investment purpose can be another powerful way to build wealth outside of the business. Real estate is unique for two reasons: It can be highly leveraged (sometimes with as little as 5 percent down payment with a 95 percent loan), and it carries with it multiple tax advantages through depreciation. While certainly highly dependent on location and purchase price, historically real estate has a lower return than the stock market with somewhat less risk—though the leverage can increase both. However, leveraging modest returns, converting the expense of lease payments into loan payments, and reducing the debt on valuable property directly builds tax-favored wealth. This can be a complex calculation with many moving parts (interest rate of the loan, down payment amount, amortization schedule, assumed appreciation of the property, and assumed cost of maintenance), so be sure to run the numbers before you make a purchase. If the property doesn't appreciate as fast as your loan interest and/or the property's upkeep is higher than expected, this approach can work against you. Thus, like most things, make sure to make a discriminating purchase and understand there may be many competing buyers, including real estate developers.

Real estate holding structures are as necessary as a seat belt. We always recommend investment or business properties be held in an entity like an LLC. Properties can be magnets for lawsuits (think slip and fall), so the primary purpose is to provide some asset protection from such events. The most common arrangement between your real estate entity and your business is a triple-net lease. A triple-net lease simply means that the tenant pays the property taxes, insurance, and maintenance. For business owners, owning their property personally through an LLC and having their business sign a lease with this entity can flow passive income through to the business owner's personal return while enjoying the benefits of property depreciation.

Especially as a business approaches a sale, the leases must be at fair market value. This means they have similar terms to what you would offer to a third-party tenant. This helps simplify negotiations with buyers and shows the true cash flow of the business. While it is common for buyers to purchase the real estate as part of the transaction, this is not always the case.

Opportunity zones: As part of the 2017 Tax Cuts and Jobs Act, a specialized tax benefit was created for real estate development within "opportunity zones." These zones are identified by the government to revitalize impoverished communities by encouraging new businesses and residences into these areas. The tax benefits are extremely generous and equally complicated, so be sure to work with an experienced attorney in this area. The benefits include the ability to defer capital gains taxes on previous sales (within strict timing guidelines) and the ability to reduce or eliminate capital gains taxes on property purchased and held within these zones, depending on the length of the holding period. Many requirements exist on the use of the property and the number of improvements necessary to qualify. It is also worth noting that many hedge funds have been created to develop land in these areas, so they can represent either a competing purchaser for the more valuable properties or an opportunity for you to participate in these funds if you meet certain investor qualifications and have an advisor with access. Hedge funds require investors to meet several criteria for income or investable assets, depending on the fund. If you're interested in putting your money in a hedge fund talk to your financial advisor.

Conservation easements: For those BHBO with environmentalism as part of their true north and holders of undeveloped land, conservation easements can be a way to preserve these properties from future development and gain a current tax deduction in the process. A conservation easement is the irrevocable (can't get it back) gift to a nonprofit land trust that gives the trust the ability to monitor and preserve the property for environmental conservation. As you are giving up some control over the development of the property through a legally binding easement, it is important to be sure you have met with and agree with the nonprofit's processes and mission. However, as this is a real gift, you can gain a meaningful tax deduction of up to 40 percent of the property's value and potentially additional state tax credits.

Traditional Wealth-Building Tools

Up to this point, I've discussed building wealth using tax-favored tools. These are incredibly useful and can greatly magnify, returns, but sometimes fewer distribution rules and high liquidity is the best option, especially when you seek maximum flexibility. Both of the following do not have complicated tax rules to limit your access to the money.

> **Managing your cash:** No discussion of wealth building can be complete without covering cash management, frequently overlooked by many business owners as the idea that keeping cash in one bank account isn't always the best balance between risk and return, especially as accounts grow. Many a business owner has watched gratefully as their statement grows as representative of their hard work, only to unwittingly leave thousands of dollars on the table and perhaps even some of the principal at risk. Cash management is simply being deliberate about maximizing the return on cash while being mindful of the risk. Is cash risky? Not in normal times, but it certainly can be when not careful. For instance, having more than $250,000 (the FDIC insured limit) in an unstable bank that failed in 2008 would have been very risky, including the potential loss of all the excess deposits. Risk is not just the chance of losing principal; it's also the inability to use the cash when it's needed. Also in 2008, we saw a cash management tool called "auction market securities" freeze up, meaning investors were unable to access their cash for months and in some cases years. Of course, bank deposits should be the foundation of a good strategy, but knowing options to increase safety and or yield is important. Following are a few ideas so you can ask good questions:
>
> - Covering excess deposits with FDIC: Many banks participate in programs that allow you to spread your

money into different banks to increase your total FDIC coverage. This can be done through CD programs (you would have many CDs of different institutions in one bank) or sweep deposit programs (your money deposited into multiple banks through your originating bank). This allows combined FDIC limits well over $250,000, sometimes $3 million or higher.

- Money markets from mutual fund companies: Even though these have no FDIC insurance and can lose value, the risk on excess holdings (also uninsured) is different from a bank deposit (which is subject to one bank's solvency). Money markets will invest-diversify into many types of short-term bond holdings, some riskier than others and sometimes paying you higher interest rates than bank deposits. Funds can invest in municipal bonds, government bonds, or even corporate bonds—which gives you a wide selection of risk/return.

- Short-term investments: If you have larger balances ($5 million or higher), it may make sense for you or an investment advisor to buy and manage the short-term instruments yourself for better control over yield, quality, and when you need the money (liquidity).

- High-quality portfolio with a line of credit: If you have adequate cash for working capital and seek higher returns for cash you are not likely to need in short term, you can invest in a diversified portfolio, including longer-term bonds, and apply for a secured line of credit against it. This allows your money the opportunity to grow at potentially higher rates, yet you can access the line of credit if an immediate cash need arises.

- Life insurance: As discussed in chapter 6, life insurance can be designed to maximize tax-favored cash value growth. If the investments within the policy are high quality (like the portfolio of the insurance company), you could receive a competitive tax-favored rate of return while maintaining the ability to borrow from policy at any time. If you need bonding, many bonding companies will even consider this a cash asset— with the interest rates you earn normally far higher.

Building Your Investment Portfolio

Compound interest works very well even within an after-tax portfolio outside of vehicles like retirement plans or 529s. Even though it is a taxable account, it doesn't necessarily mean you'll pay a lot of tax. You do not pay taxes on positions that grow before you sell them, so limiting trading can limit taxes. Capital gains taxes on positions held more than a year are also at lower rates than income (in 2022 for married filing jointly, the tax is 0 percent up to $83,350 of adjusted gross income, 15 percent if income is less than $517,200, and 20 percent if higher—versus 37 percent highest marginal income tax rate). Income from dividends is usually taxed at the lower capital gains rates. Finally, municipal bonds can provide a source of tax-free income.

A balanced portfolio (using stocks, bonds, cash, and other asset classes) can provide a competitive return depending on the risk you want to take. The more risk, the higher the percent of stocks and the higher the potential return. I usually suggest targeting less risk in after-tax accounts as you may use the money sooner, which could happen at a time when markets are down.

I will discuss more about investing in chapter 10 (after an exit), as many business owners find themselves uncomfortable moving from managing a business to managing a portfolio after a sale.

Intelligent Use of Charitable Giving

Perhaps no other area better defines the BHBO than their involvement with charities and their communities. While any type of help to charities can be laudable, being deliberate about the type and manner of gifting can make huge differences to the net effect of the gift. This section will arm the BHBO with ways to make gifts in the most tax-effective manner.

Gifts of appreciated assets: While giving cash is simple and benefits the charity, it is rarely the best way to make a sizable gift if you hold appreciated assets. As the charity would not pay taxes on the sale of appreciated assets, you can avoid the capital gains taxes *and* get the charitable deduction, a much more efficient way to gift. In other words, you are completely avoiding the tax on the growth of your stock while still gaining the tax deduction from the gift. Appreciated assets can be stock in your business, real estate, publicly traded stocks or even artwork. I will discuss more advanced techniques of making gifts of assets like business stock and real estate in later chapters, but here I will focus on liquid/easily divided assets like individual publicly traded stocks.

Consider an example. You want to make a gift to a charity of $12,500 and are trying to choose between gifting stock and cash. Let's say you purchased 100 shares of Apple at $5, for $500 and it's now worth $125 a share or $12,500. If you gift the $12,500 cash, you only get the tax deduction. However, if you give these 10 shares to the charity, you still receive the deduction *and* the charity pays no tax on selling the shares, so they have full use of $12,500. Your $12,000 in capital gain just became tax-free If you still want to own Apple, you then repurchase the Apple stock (if it fits your objectives) and your new taxable basis has increased to $12,500.

Donor-advised funds: The 2017 tax act dramatically increased the standard deduction from $12,700 for a married couple in 2017 to $25,100 in 2021. One intent was to simplify tax returns so fewer would itemize since total deductions lower than this standard deduction can't be used. Still, it has the unintended effect of making charitable deductions useless for tax purposes if below the standard deduction. Many charities have been concerned this would hurt charitable giving, but happily, there is no evidence of that happening. If you make regular annual gifts to a charity, there is a nifty tool to aggregate regular annual gifts into one year to use the deductions on your tax return: donor-advised funds (DAF). These are charitable foundations preestablished by local communities, mutual fund managers, or wealth management firms that allow donors to establish their own named sub-account (like the "Jones Family Foundation") and then ask the DAF to make grants to their chosen charities in future years if it is a qualifying charity. For instance, say the family makes $15,000 annual gifts to their church, which is too small to deduct on their tax return. If they made a $60,000 gift in one year (which would more than qualify as deductible), then the DAF would contribute the $15,000 to charity each year following. Net result? At least a $30,000 tax deduction they otherwise would not have enjoyed. The previous two techniques can easily be combined. Make a gift of appreciated stock to a DAF, avoid the capital gains, and utilize the higher deduction in the year of gift! In the previous example, the family would gift $60,000 of appreciated stock(s), gaining the deduction and avoiding the capital gains taxes and gaining a $34,900 deduction otherwise lost plus avoiding the capital gains on the appreciated stock gift. In the highest bracket and zero basis, that's over $20,000 in saved taxes. Being smart in this manner can encourage more gifting!

Qualified charitable distribution: If you have money in a traditional IRA or 401k, the government eventually wants to tax it. One tool it uses to do so is called "required minimum distributions," which forces you to take distributions once you reach

72 years old (the SECURE Act moved it from 70.5 for those who are not yet that age). This means you are forced to take a distribution based on the value of all your accounts and your age, so the forced amount increases every year. Rather than take this distribution, you can direct up to $100,000 of it to a charity or DAF and avoid income taxes on this distribution.

Charitable trusts: Several types of charitable trusts can be useful ways to combine charitable giving with tax savings, depending on our income goals:

> **Need income during lifetime—charitable remainder trust (CRT):** Have highly appreciated property/stock/business and still need income from the asset? A CRT is a way to defer capital gains taxes on the sale, gain a meaningful tax deduction, and keep the entire value of the asset providing income to you or your family during your lifetime or a period of years. After either the term ends or after the trust beneficiaries pass away, the remaining assets go to charity. I will discuss them in more detail during the next chapter on exits as corporate stock can be a perfect asset used to fund a CRT. For now, the following is an example using a gifted stock with a low basis: Let's say two shares of BRK (Berkshire Hathaway) were gifted by parents who bought the stock when it was worth only $50,000, and it's now grown to $600,000. Berkshire doesn't pay a dividend (income), and you would like to diversify the position and create more ability to create income at retirement, especially if you're in a cargo business and you expect the exit to be modest. A "net income with makeup charitable remainder unitrust" (NIMCRUT—don't we love our acronyms!) is established, and the stock is gifted to the trust. Assuming

a 5 percent payout is established, and that the donor is 50 years old, the donor gets approximately a $150,000 deduction, the trust is diversified with no taxes, and the entire $600,000 remains to grow and eventually provide income when the donor retires—5 percent of the future value (if it grows to $1.2 million in ten years, it will provide approximately $60,000 in annual income). It would have deferred over $125,000 in capital gains taxes at the highest marginal rates in South Carolina and saved almost $60,000 in income taxes. And the charity receives a meaningful lump sum at the end of the term, likely over $1 million if the trust performance can exceed 5 percent. The donor enjoyed higher income to help fund a retirement lifestyle than otherwise expected from the position because of the tax savings and made a nice contribution to charity after their death.

Large estate looking to reduce taxes and provide donation to charity—charitable lead trust (CLT): CLTs are more frequently used as estate planning techniques when there is charitable intent, the estate is larger than the unified credit, and there is a desire for assets to go to family beneficiaries. They are usually established after the parents pass away and provide an income to a charity for a specified term, then at the end of that term, the remaining assets transfer to the family (usually in a trust). Yep, it's complicated. But the result can be a significant reduction in estate taxes, which currently have the highest rate of 40 percent. Famously, Jacqueline Kennedy Onassis (JFK's wife) established a CLT for her estate, helping the family avoid millions in taxes while also paying out millions to charities—CLTs are sometimes called "Jackie O" trusts.

State and federal tax credits: It is important to be aware that each state/municipality has many tax credits that are unique but can mean significant refunds. Solar credits, hiring credits, moving into a new area, and expanding your operations are all examples. Similarly, federal tax credits also may exist to help and change frequently. Be sure to rely on your tax team to avoid leaving money on the table.

Family Business Ideas

So how do you enjoy the flight within the unique canard of a family business? How does the BHBO with a desire to help their family draw appropriate boundaries to help promote self-sufficiency? What are the tools available for governance, communication of values, and potentially reducing taxes unique to family businesses?

These topics are the subjects of many books, seminars, associations, and white papers since these problems are universally felt in family businesses, which represent such a large percent of all closely held entities. In this section, I will share resources I have found useful for clients and encourage readers to continue the never-ending process of learning what works well for their business and their family.

Governance

Being a parent is difficult. Being a parent with family members in the business can be even harder. The unique part about running a family business is that you must deal with the emotions and responsibilities of running a business while having business partners or employees who are family members. The quick solution to all the issues that arise from family businesses is to try and avoid favoritism. Of course, that is not only far easier said than done, and it isn't always the best solution for the BHBO looking to help family and perhaps groom a family member for succession. The fine line between helping and enablement is why many family businesses have a trained counselor as an essential part of their team. The risk is that enablement becomes too embedded such that it hurts business profitability, or worse, it hurts the work ethic of family members and/or creates discontent from non-family employees. Following are a few ways to steer away from these outcomes.

> **Family mission statement:** As discussed in chapter 1, mission statements can help a family business remain focused on the family's core values and objectives. This helps guide decision-making, especially through difficult times where there may be conflict.

> **Family meetings:** Family meetings in the context of business governance are the most common way to provide governance and promote good decision-making within a family business. These meetings can cover a wide variety of topics depending on the age of family members, their involvement in the business, and the level of control ultimately sought by the founders of the business. When children are young, having family meetings to help educate on financial decisions, business decisions, or charitable involvement can be a tremendous learning experience. As they grow, giving them limited decision-making in meetings (like management of properties or charitable gifts) can be a good learning experience. Making gifts to them within the context of the mission statement and corporate profitability can also be a great way to allow mistakes to be made and from them to learn from them. Ultimately, a family business intent on family transition will have family meetings like that of corporate board meetings where open communication and voting are shared.

Resources: As I mentioned, the governance of family business is a topic of ample resources. Following is a list you may find helpful in this important topic:

- Many universities have programs or forums on family businesses; check out a school near you.
- The Family Business Network is an international non-profit dedicated to providing resources/networking to family businesses.
- Most peer networking organizations, such as Vistage, have family business groups or message boards dedicated to this area.

Following are a few books I believe useful: *Every Family's Business: 12 Common Sense Questions to Protect Your Wealth* by Thomas William Deans and *In the Company of Family—How to Thrive When Business is Personal* by Melissa Mitchell-Blitch (also a Charlestonian). The *Harvard Business Review* also has many articles on the topic.

Gifting: Most of the previously discussed ideas on gifting would apply easily to a family-run business as well. However, unique to family businesses is the use of gifts during your lifetime both as a means of helping family members and potentially reducing estate taxes. Since the taxes on gifts likely goes up dramatically in 2026, as previously discussed, gifting may be an especially timely strategy in the next few years.

Gifting mechanisms (usually for estates over $12 million under current law or worried about changes): Gifting to children/grandchildren is usually done to reduce the value of an estate, to reduce estate taxes, to gradually shift control to the family under an orderly succession plan, and because you love your children/family and want to help them! Following are techniques used to leverage gifting:

Annual exclusion: Each parent can make a "gift of a present interest" (meaning beneficiaries need the right to use/enjoy the gift, even if they save it instead). One annual exclusion of $16,000 (in 2022) can be used from each spouse to each child, so $32,000 can be gifted to one child each year.

GRATs: Grantor-retained annuity trusts provide income to the "grantor" (the person establishing the rust) for a period of years, after which the trust assets go to the beneficiaries. The income reduces the value of the gift, and all the growth occurs in the beneficiary's name. However, the grantor must outlive the trust term, or the gift is reversed.

IDGT (intentionally defective grantor trust): These complicated trusts are used to reduce estate taxes on assets that generate income and are likely to grow in value. It is a trust set up by the grantor (usually a parent) that makes the grantor continue to pay taxes on any taxable income within the trust. The beneficiaries (usually the kids), eventually receive the gifted asset, hopefully when the asset has grown higher in value. The benefit of the trust is that the gift tax is based on the value of the gift when it is established—all future appreciation isn't subject to estate taxes. Plus, the taxes being paid by the grantor are not taxable gifts, further reducing the estate.

Irrevocable life insurance trust (ILIT): These trusts can be used in a variety of ways to avoid estate taxes on insurance proceeds and protect these assets for the beneficiaries. The most common use of these trusts has been to provide liquidity for an estate that is subject to estate taxes. Assets held within an ILIT are not part of a taxable estate, and life insurance pays a tax-free death benefit. For example, if an illiquid estate were subject to $5 million in taxes, a $5 million policy could be purchased, the tax-free proceeds of which could then purchase stock in the family business, giving the estate cash to pay the taxes while preserving ownership for the family. These trusts can also be used to leverage the tax laws to increase the size of an estate that reaches family members. For example, if parents are confident that they have more than they need, they can take extra money they're certain they'll never spend and place it into an ILIT. This ILIT then provides tax-free growth and is not part of the taxable estate—leaving the kids more than if the money were left in the estate since it is tax-free.

For larger estates in today's extremely low-rate environment, it is even possible to borrow to pay all the premiums, as many banks view life insurance as high-quality collateral. This is called "premium financing" and can work well when the return on the life policy is higher than the cost of the loan, which has been more utilized in the current low-rate environment. Of course, if the policy does not perform well, the loan amount can eat up some or all the death benefits, making this a riskier strategy.

Ralph Waldo Emerson said, "Life is a journey, not a destination." This chapter covered dozens of techniques to help make this ride smooth and help you avoid those dreaded thunderstorms. With an understanding of your goals/values, a basic understanding of what is available, and the help of a good team, you can utilize select tools majestically to enjoy every step of your journey as you've built your business, built your wealth, protected it, and taken care of your passengers. We are nearing the end of this book's flight. It is time to start preparing the cabin for landing.

Chapter 8

Preparing for Landing: The Exit

"I DON'T BELIEVE IN DYING. IT'S BEEN DONE. I'M WORKING ON A NEW EXIT. BESIDES, I CAN'T DIE NOW—I'M BOOKED!"
—GEORGE BURNS

All pilots understand that takeoffs and landings are the most dangerous part of any flight. It's the same in business, with failed takeoffs and crash landings the riskiest parts of running a business. Only a small percentage of companies survive more than a few years. Selling a business and steering a safe landing at your destination is frequently the largest and most important transition you'll navigate as an owner. To avoid a rough or crash landing, preparation is key. There's a lot that can go wrong. You could land at the wrong destination (by choosing the wrong type of exit or wrong timing). You could run out of runway (by not asking for a sufficient purchase price consistent with your goals). Or you could land with a group of angry, unwieldy passengers (by choosing the wrong successor). In this chapter, I'll help you, as a BHBO, to grease the landing, as we pilots say.

Your Pre-Landing Checklist

For pilots, a pre-landing checklist guides them through the steps to make sure their aircraft has all the navigation and communication equipment set accurately to the correct destination. It also familiarizes the pilot with the best approach and configuration for the landing as well as prepares the passengers for what's to come. A good checklist sets everyone on the plane up for an optimal landing experience. In business, a pre-exit checklist has similar goals and benefits. A solid pre-exit checklist should cover the following:

- Choose the best timing for an exit.
- Document personal and professional goals for the business exit.
- Determine the range of business value that can be expected.
- Drive up the value of their business before the exit.
- Determine the best and most likely exit scenarios.
- Choose key players, including an intermediary where needed, to help execute the exit.
- Make sure business documents are prepared and organized.
- Complete personal planning.

The rest of this chapter will dive deeper into each item on the checklist.

Exit Timing: Prerequisites

Planning for the timing and terms of a business exit can often be difficult for owners. These decisions are often deeply personal and influenced by the various scenarios that owners play out in their minds while navigating the challenging years of running and growing their businesses. All your blood, sweat, and tears can shape a sacred vision in your heart and mind—making it difficult to plan for the inevitable departure from your "baby" that is required by most exits. That's why it is so important that you shape the terms of your exit. Consider these questions as initial ways to determine if you and your business are ready to start planning for an exit:

Can you take a long vacation without your business imploding? While it might seem surprising, this is the most critical question to ask yourself as an owner before an exit. Your answer serves as guidance as to whether your business is ready for exit planning. If your business would implode without you, much work needs to be done. Most exits do involve a transition period in which the owner transfers knowledge, processes, and skills to a buyer. However, no buyer wants to purchase a business that has a high risk of revenue dropping, suppliers walking away, or some hidden but key piece of knowledge hurting the business if these rely on the original owner remaining in the business. Thus, it is important to be mindful of how a potential buyer will view your business and to groom employees to take on your job functions. Yes, it is good to train others to take over at least some of your job.

Are you mentally ready for an exit? It can be difficult to leave something you have spent your entire life building—even if you started with the intention to sell. Being mentally ready for an exit involves preparing for the next phase of your life, which might include retirement, charitable work, or perhaps starting another business. A great way to tell is by spending time imagining what you would do and how you would feel if you were financially secure, but no longer had your business. Does it feel good? Are you not yet ready to let go?

Are the financial goals for your next phase of life in reach? Your financial plan will help you determine if you are financially prepared for life after your business sale. Ideally, you should set a timeframe for your exit based on your financial plan. Of course, the value of the business will have a significant impact on its readiness to sell. There is also a possibility that you will receive an unsolicited offer on your business. Your financial plan will let you know if the offer will be enough to reach your goals. I will discuss both financial and non-financial goals of an exit in the next section.

Is your business ready for a sale? Being ready for a sale includes several items, among them are the following:

- The documentation items discussed in chapter 4 should mostly be in place.
- The business should be consistently profitable and show a positive trend over the preceding three years.
- Personal expenses should be cleaned off the books.

Is your exit strategy feasible in the current economic climate? Pilots spend hours of training preparing for landing in bad weather. They have learned that even if all the needles and gauges line up, it's best to go around the storm rather than try to land in inclement weather. It is the same with exits: The environment should reasonably accommodate the type of exit you seek. The market of willing buyers, the ability to obtain financing, the amount of cash available on the balance sheets of potential buyers, the economy's impact on your ongoing profitability can all be significantly impacted by the economic environment, which is firmly *not* in your control. Recognizing favorable environments before you are ready for the exit can drastically increase your potential purchase price. For these reasons, you should always operate your business as though you are getting ready to sell.

Personal Goals of Exit

The BHBO tends to have a different approach to forming and executing their personal goals of the exit. Many books have been written about maximizing the exit value. These books should be of great interest and merit to you as a BHBO. However, sometimes the absolute maximum value and your personal goals may not be fully aligned. As discussed earlier, sometimes the tax benefits of an ESOP can outweigh a higher exit price. Sometimes a business owner wants to maintain some control over their business for themselves or family members. In this case, the owner may be willing to give up some value in return for this control. There may also be times when an owner is willing to sell to a particular buyer (maybe even employees) at a slightly lower price if it helps maintain the culture, mission, or vision the owner has for the business. Most of these decisions are made when they have ensured their own lifestyle goals are met. If you are a fighter jet–type business, the exit strategy can especially accelerate meeting all these goals. However, you must figure out the financial exit number needed before moving on to the next items in the checklist.

Your Exit Number

Chapter 4 discussed the business owner's financial plan and how critical this instrument is for your success; here is where it is more important than ever. Within the plan, you will input both your lifestyle goals as needs; these include retirement income, health care, housing, travel, and support for children like college. Then aspirational goals you'll enter as wants—charitable giving, family gifting, community involvement, starting another business, or even things like building a family vacation home—fit under this category. From this, you will then determine a range of what you need from an exit. The low end funds your needs; the high end funds all of your wants.

As a BHBO, you'll include needs and wants that are financial and non-financial, professional and personal. Your non-financial exit goals will not be written in your financial plan but are very important to the BHBO as they sometimes have an impact on the purchase price of your chosen exit. Even if they may reduce the price, they may still be worthwhile as you may place a significant value on them, and/or your expected purchase price already exceeds what you need to meet your financial goals. The blend of financial and non-financial goals can help you determine the best type of exit. Ask yourself these questions:

- How long are you willing to work in the business post-exit?
- Are you OK answering to a new boss?
- How important is maintaining your business's culture?
- Are there family members or key employees within the business that you would prefer as buyers and/or successor management?
- Are there any parts of the business you would want to see maintained (employees, product/service lines, vendor relationships, etc.)?

If some of these items are important to you, you will need to determine if you can accept any reduction in exit price. Knowing your financial exit number can help you determine if you can afford these goals as part of the exit.

Once you have both your financial and non-financial goals set, it is critically important to write them down. Writing them down will help you stay on track during negotiations and the closing process, which will almost always force you to make decisions affecting these terms. This helps you know what you can and cannot accept during your exit.

Determining Exit Value

Ah, valuations! Many books have been written on how to identify the drivers of valuing a business, which is both art and science. However, this book will focus on the high-level concepts you need to consider when contextually planning your personal goals.

The IRS calls "fair market value" the "price that would be agreed on between a willing buyer and a willing seller, with neither being required to act and both having reasonable knowledge of the relevant facts." I included this frequently quoted definition because, ultimately, price is determined by whatever a buyer and seller agree is the right amount versus some magical formula. However, formulas are useful in setting guidelines of value. Analyzing industry comparables on your specific business and identifying the type of business you are operating, a cargo or fighter, is essential to discovering your exit value.

There are three main drivers of value: recurring profits, growth rates, and book value. These are the most important items to focus on when trying to increase the value of your business.

> **Book value:** Think of book value as the low end of your business's valuation. It is the liquidation value of your business if you were to close the doors and walk away, as you should be able to get at least the net value of all your business's assets. Naturally, this shouldn't be the preferred price! However, a business with a significant book value (owns valuable assets held by the business) will usually be able to add some of this value to the overall purchase price that is calculated with the other methods of recurring profits or growth rates.

> **Recurring profits:** Recurring profits are essential to both the cargo and fighter and are usually defined as EBITDA— earnings before income taxes, depreciation, and amortization. The reason many use this number as the basis for value is that this somewhat accurately reflects the pre-tax-free cash flow of the business. While the EBITDA is found on most financial statements, for valuation purposes it is common to adjust EBITDA to try and identify the profits likely to be enjoyed by the new buyer. These usually drive up the value considerably as owner perks are identified. These important adjustments include items like the following:

- **Adjusting owners' or family members' salaries:** If, for instance, the owner's salary is $1 million a year, the adjustment may assume a new CEO could be hired at $250,000 per year. This adjustment adds $750,000 to earnings since it more accurately reflects benefits of ownership versus salary.

- **Adjusting leases:** If the owner leases their personally owned property to business, an adjustment may be made upward or downward to make sure it reflects the fair market value of the lease. Sometimes these leases can be older and haven't been updated in a while. It is common for a buyer to purchase real estate along with the business, but this adjustment helps to accurately reflect the value of both assets

- **Removing nonrecurring expenses or revenue:** These expenses are anything that are not commonly expected in an annual budget such as a large purchase that may have been motivated by generating tax deductions or a large one-time sale unlikely to be replicated. This helps the buyer have a more realistic expectation of future earnings. Certain code sections, such as section 179, allow owners to accelerate deductions during the year of purchase—which can allow the purchase of a large piece of equipment to eliminate taxable profits in the year of purchase. Spreading this cost over time will more accurately reflect the profits for the potential buyer.

- **Removing discretionary expenses:** This sometimes includes items paid for partially by the business that may include a personal benefit for the owner and their family. Company car, cell phone bills, and some business travel are all examples of such discretionary expenses.

As you can see, a buyer isn't just interested in profits. A buyer is interested in profits that will continue after they purchase your business.

Growth: Business growth is important to both the cargo and fighter but is much more vital for the fighter since this type of business may not have the same level of profitability as the cargo. Growth represents to a buyer *future* potential earnings. Growth of the business for valuation purposes is most frequently identified by the growth in normalized revenue. Like the adjustments to earnings discussed in the previous section, normalization is taking out nonrecurring revenue items. This measurement of earnings isn't always the sole measure of growth. Some industries will track other items more intently than revenue if those items are likely to lead to future higher revenue. For example, many software companies are more concerned about the growth in subscribers than current revenue growth since the subscribers can lead to higher revenues.

Now that I've covered the main drivers of value, let's discuss how it pertains to a cargo and a fighter. Depending on the business, the value will be based on a continuum between recurring profits and growth, with perhaps an extra amount for any valuable equipment within the book value. While a small number of cargo businesses are valued on a multiple of gross revenues, most businesses are valued as a multiple of the recurring profits previously described: adjusted EBITDA. In other words, the value of a business is a "multiple" (such as five) times the adjusted EBITDA. Typically, the higher the growth rate of a business, the higher the multiple. However, some businesses with extremely rapid growth can have a negative EBITDA number as their free cash flow is invested into the business to further accelerate growth. In these cases, a value is based on what a buyer predicts the future profits will be once the owners turn on the profits switch—meaning managing for-profits versus growth. For instance, Amazon showed little to no profits for years yet clearly had built plenty of value! Of course, companies like this are much more difficult to value. Thus, cargo businesses typically have lower valuations. This is because they usually have lower growth, and less of the recurring profits may transfer to the buyer.

It is also common for larger businesses to have higher multiples since larger businesses tend to be more stable. This is one reason that some private equity firms will consolidate businesses in a specific industry. The reason they often consolidate is that if they buy ten companies with a $5 million-adjusted EBITDA company and a 5-time multiple (costing $250 million), they could streamline operations and then resell one company with a $50 million adjusted EBITDA with a higher 8-time multiple ($400 million sales price) and make a hefty gain purely from the higher multiple.

One of the best estimates of value an owner can find is a range of multiples for their type and size of business. Talking to an investment banker, business broker, or industry trade group can give you a good idea of the range of values for your business. Alternatively, a formal valuation from an appropriately qualified CPA can both give you a range of values and a value that can be used to transact some succession activities.

Increasing Business Value: Converting Knowledge into Action

Now that I've identified how a buyer will view your business value, let's discuss some high-level ways to increase this value for both cargos and fighters. Here, again, many books and consultants outline successful strategies for increasing value, dependent on your type of business. If you are within a few years of a potential exit, it can be worthwhile to consider adding one of these consultants to your team. Your focus should be on increasing the value drivers: recurring and transferrable profits and growth.

Increasing Recurring and Transferrable Profits

- **Operate for maximizing profits and not minimize tax:** Frequently, business owners buy a piece of equipment, invest in a software program, or otherwise accelerate expenses to reduce a tax bill before year's end. When approaching an exit, it is important to spend only as appropriate to maintain or help accelerate growth.

- **Remove or reduce expenses that may have a personal element:** The process of adjusting your income is something you want to do before seeking a buyer. There may be some element of increasing EBITDA by doing so to increase profits, but it is far more attractive to a buyer to have them removed from the corporate books. A daughter working within the business accustomed to a corporate vehicle may be a problem if new ownership decides not to provide the vehicle.

- **Wherever possible, remove yourself from the business:** I probably sound like a broken record by now, but a buyer will only purchase what will transfer to them. If customers are likely to bail if you are no longer present or the business falls apart in your absence, it will hurt your exit price.

- **Seek opportunities to maximize growth and profits:** This is the broadest area where a consultant can add the most value, though you may intuitively know the things you have been postponing for the right time. Now is the right time. I have been amazed watching owners crank up their EBIDTA once they understand the reasoning.

Determining the Best and Most Likely Exit Scenarios

I am excited about this section of the book because few resources provide business owners with all the information on all the types of internal and external exits and how they related to personal goals. Especially for the BHBO with multiple goals, having this information can be crucial to enjoying the next phase in their life and helping them reach their destination.

As you consider whether an internal or external exit is best, there are a few points to keep in context:

- **Tax implications:** Capital gains versus income taxes: It's not what you make, it's what you keep. Capital gains apply to the sale of a capital asset—such as business stock—and are generally at lower rates (20 percent typical long-term rate in 2022). Income taxes can be on the purchase of assets you have depreciated, such as goodwill or equipment, and are at a much higher tax rate of up to 37 percent. These do not include state taxes or Obamacare taxes. A buyer will want to purchase the assets as they then have the option of restarting the deductible depreciation cycle. This creates a natural conflict between buyer and seller between a stock purchase and an asset purchase.
- **Impacts on lifestyle:** How much control will you maintain after the transaction? Will you have to answer to someone else, and how will it affect your corporate culture?
- **Legal implications:** What liabilities will you retain versus transfer to the new owner?
- **Valuation implications:** How do the exit options under consideration vary in likely sales price?
- **Consistent with goals:** Does the exit align with the goals that you wrote down from the previous section?

Types of Exits

There are several types of planned and unplanned exits that every BHBO should understand. The more you know about your choices in either situation, the better equipped you'll be to optimize your outcome. Let's dive in.

Unplanned Exit.

Everyone exits their business eventually, either in a planned or unplanned fashion. It is important to consider what happens to your business if you haven't made plans or you end up with a long-term disability that prevents you from working or in the event of your death. Types of unplanned exits usually follow this sequence:

1. Owner departs the business.
2. Suppliers, employees, and clients question the long-term viability of business but wait and see as successor management is determined.
3. Surviving shareholder(s) (usually family member without business experience) tries to decide whether to sell or keep the business. This is an intensely emotional decision compounded with the recent loss. It is not uncommon for employees to lobby the survivor into continuing the business (keeping their jobs) even if it's not in the best interest of protecting value left in the business.
4. Successor managers are chosen, and customers, suppliers, and employees will evaluate the new management cautiously. With the ensuing uncertainty, it is rare to retain all of them—likely attrition from each takes its toll on the business.
5. Bankers evaluate successor management to determine if loans are to be continued or called—if they haven't already been closed as the owner usually personally guaranteed loans.
6. The business is either sold/liquidated or continues to operate as a going concern with new management.

It is imperative that you have a plan in place for any kind of exit—planned or unexpected. A clear plan can help you face the significant headwinds for a favorable outcome. Without one, you will likely defray the value of the business either through forced liquidation or slow death, all while burdening your survivors and those remaining in the business.

Planned Exits During Your Lifetime.

Happily, business owners most likely will live to an old age and can choose the type of exit that is best for themselves and those they care about. The main difference between these planned exits is the source of funding your buyout: either internal or external. Internal buyouts are funded by employee funds, excess business cash flow, or family gifting strategies. External buyouts are funded with money from outside parties.

> **Internal exits.** Internal exits involve a planned succession to family members, business partners, or employees who possess the ability and interest to manage the business after your departure. Internal exits generally have more favorable tax implications, usually allowing for you to maintain a great deal of control through the process. They typically have lower valuations than selling to an outside party. These exits are usually planned over several years as you slowly transition out of your business but still allow you to continue to work until you transition your business at your desired time or death. While these can be used for either the fighter or cargo, they are much more common for cargo and family businesses.
>
> A note about internal exits for cargo businesses: Although investors who are family members may be more patient than others, many outside investors seek

a liquidity event at some point. Some investors hold purchased businesses as a source of income much like a portfolio of income-producing real estate. Because of this, internal exits are not ideal for the exit-seeking investor as the valuations and time to exit may be lower and longer, but they shouldn't be discounted. An internal transition to competent successor management can be a reliable way to create liquidity for patient outside investors.

The key requirement for all internal exits is assigning competent successor management. Identifying, training, and transitioning responsibilities to a team that can take over is a process that takes years of deliberate planning. The skill of your successor has a major bearing on the valuation of your exit, the reliability of business income streams, and the ability to obtain financing. For instance, if a successor team struggles to make payments on the note they used to purchase your business, you may end up back in the business as a condition of the default.

Training leadership is far beyond the scope of this book, but good resources are available in most communities. Consulting firms focusing on leadership, peer groups, and knowledgeable boards are valuable resources to help new management. However, at the end of the day, being willing to mentor successors and transition responsibilities to new leadership is your responsibility and the most important part of the process. Even though others can provide useful ideas, nobody can replace your deliberate thought in the type of training most useful to run your business. It is important to keep an open mind as nobody will ever run the business exactly as you do now.

Buy/sell agreement as testamentary (at death) succession plan. Succession plans can be ideal if you love what you do or have a family business you hope to transition to your heirs in later years of life. Of course, the most imperative point of this strategy is that you will not have a liquidity event during your lifetime. Thus, you will need to plan on having assets outside of the business or having the business continue to pay you an income.

Since the business will be transitioned at death, the funding is normally through a life insurance policy that is coordinated with a buy/sell agreement, as I discussed in chapter 6. Family businesses, in particular, are good candidates for this strategy when founders hope to continue control and the toolbox of estate planning attorneys can be maximized.

Management buyout. Once successor management has been identified and has proven both the talent and interest, the planning for a management buyout can begin. Structuring these buyouts is usually driven by three items: the financial capability of successor management to fund a buyout, whether successor management is family, and the acceptable timeline for you to receive your exit payments.

Ideally, successor management has the means or ability to obtain financing to fund a buyout. This is preferred as it allows for more favorable long-term capital gains tax treatment, it increases the basis for the buyers, and it removes you from having to be a financial guarantor sooner. It is helpful to start speaking with bankers or other sources of funding earlier (outside investors) to determine if it is feasible. Setting the goals of these management buyout structures are fairly simple as you can negotiate the purchase price (usually with the initial guideline of an accountant business valuation), then arrange the terms of the purchase that meet the goals of the buyer and seller. An installment sale over a period of years is most common, allowing for the gradual transition of leadership to new buyers. It's also common for the purchase to be layered out in phases, specifically one purchase for new management to have skin in the game, then another purchase where control is ceded. Fifty-one percent ownership represents controlling interest with most companies, but sometimes different shares of stocks can be used. For instance, a "manager managed" LLC is controlled by the managers versus the members (owners). In this case, a manager with a 2 percent member interest could conceivably still control the company. The bottom line is that you have flexibility on the timing of the change in control. Of course, control is worth money—you will not receive the full price for a business until control is ceded (called a control premium). Very frequently, successor management does not have the financial means to fund a buyout. In these instances, it can be beneficial to incorporate qualified, nonqualified benefit programs and entity stock purchases to create more tax-efficient funding. Even though it is a simple approach, paying out a bonus to help fund a buyout has two main problems:

- It is tax inefficient as the buyer will pay income taxes on the bonus, then you will pay capital gains taxes on the purchase. In the worst case, well over 50 percent in taxes are paid to help fund your purchase.

- It does not obligate the buyer to purchase your stock.

In order to significantly reduce the tax impact and create the purchase obligation, it can make more sense to use several other tools in concert with your team and goals to help reduce the tax of the transaction. Following are some ideas in order of increasing tax efficiency:

> **Nonqualified plans.** As you might recall from the previous chapter, a nonqualified plan is a type of benefit program with tremendous flexibility and is usually designed for senior executives. In the context of an exit plan, you can create a plan for the new management team that helps them accrue financial benefits they are obligated to use to purchase your stock. As vesting schedules and terms are flexible, this can be one way to help an employee fund a purchase while tying them financially to the company. The downside is that employees will pay income taxes on the benefits and the business cannot deduct payments until the benefit is actually paid out (versus accrued) to employees. This can still be an expensive event though you can defer the tax until the buyout is scheduled to occur. Thus, I do not recommend this or bonus plans in general as the only tool for an employee buyout.

> **Qualified plans.** If you plan on using corporate dollars to help employees fund your buyout, qualified plans are much more tax efficient. As you recall, qualified plans are the general term for company retirement plans that "qualify" for added tax benefits, but they must meet stringent testing guidelines. The benefit to you is that part of your buyout compensation can be tax-deductible to the company and tax-deferred to

you. This significantly reduces the tax compared to the high taxation of a nonqualified bonus/purchase structure. However, the demographics of your company need to fit a certain fact pattern. The company should be small (less than around 30 employees) and have a high ratio of highly compensated to non-highly compensated employees. These plans will significantly reduce the value of your business as you are paying out all the profits to yourself through these plans. However, it doesn't matter how you are paid, as long as you are paid! Plus, this helps to increase the tax efficiency of the net amount you are paid.

Stock redemptions. A stock redemption is when the company purchases stock directly from you, reducing the number of shares you own and making stock owned by other shareholders grow in value. Incorporating stock redemptions as part of an overall buyout structure can further reduce the overall tax burden on the transaction if complicated rules are followed. For example, let's say you own 1,000 shares of stock in your company, and the next owner purchases 100 shares from you. Now you own 90 percent, and they own 10 percent. Now let's have the company purchase 798 more shares from you. This leaves you with 102 outstanding shares and the new owner with 100—or 51 percent/49 percent. If structured correctly, you would have only paid capital gains taxes on both transactions and the new owner has significantly increased their percent ownership in the company. Taken in the publicly traded context, these are "share buybacks." Share buybacks occur when a company purchases its own stock to bolster the stock price for the remaining shareholders. However, family businesses should be wary that family attribution rules can re-characterize these redemptions as dividends, a horrible outcome. Thus, proper counsel is critical.

Your team can help you pick and choose from each of these pieces of the puzzle in a way that fits your company demographics, helps you reduce taxation, helps you appropriately incentivize successor management, and allows you to cede control with the timing that fits your goals.

The Ultimate Management Buyout Tax Tool: The ESOP—Employee Stock Ownership Plan.

ESOPs are a form of qualified retirement plans that invest primarily in the stock of the sponsoring company. Thus, they create a buyer for an owner's stock when one may not otherwise exist, and employees become "beneficial owners" (meaning they have limited voting rights) in the stock. In essence, a retirement trust purchases stock from the owner (financed by a bank or the company itself), and then the trust reallocates this stock to employees in accordance with retirement plan rules. The initial purchase can be tax-deferred (deferring or avoiding capital gains taxes), the allocation to employees is tax-deductible (generating deductions on the business purchase/finance), and a 100 percent ESOP-owned company (S corporation) pays no income taxes. You read that right: It is almost tax-free. I love ESOPs. And I hate them. I love them because Congress has created these massive tax incentives for them since ESOPs can create real retirement wealth for employees and elegantly transition ownership to successor management. They can help significantly leverage the excess cash flow of a business for succession or acquisition. I hate them because they are complicated and have real pitfalls for businesses if not administered properly. Why do I call an ESOP the ultimate management buyout tool? Consider the following:

- An owner sale to an ESOP defers capital gains taxes on the sale if diversifying proceeds into a specially managed portfolio. The code section (1042) requires the company to be a C corporation and the re-purchased portfolio to be in US stocks and bonds to defer the capital gains tax. Often, conversion to a C corporation is recommended before an ESOP.

- Current law includes a step-up in the basis of capital assets, like stock, at death—which avoids capital gains taxes. Thus, if this portfolio is maintained until death (you could live off the income from the portfolio), the step-up in basis at death eliminates capital gains from the sale of a business, making it a tax-free sale.

- The business can deduct both the interest and the principal from the financing of the purchase. This is significantly more tax-efficient than the company or employees purchasing your stock directly, which is not deductible by the company.

- Once the entire purchase has been consummated, a company can be converted to an S corporation, which as mentioned before would make the company nearly tax-free. This could help cash flow if the company helped finance the transaction (maybe even allowing for an earlier payoff to you) but eventually becomes a huge benefit to the eventual owners. This is why many ESOPs start as C corporations and eventually are converted to S.

To recap, the sale can be tax-free, the financing is fully deductible, and the company post-transaction then can be tax-exempt. Compare this to the bonus-funded employee buyout with taxes potentially reaching over 50 percent! This means your purchase price could be approaching half that of a traditional purchase for you to net the same amount of money. ESOPs are one of the most powerful tax tools within the tax code.

So why doesn't everyone do an ESOP for management buyouts? Here are some of the administrative issues that must be considered:

- The purchase absolutely must be a fair price (independently valued). ESOPs do not have an unrelated buyer and seller. They have an employer (the owner) selling to all employees (represented by the retirement trust). Since owners have the natural incentive to sell at a higher price, regulators watch to ensure the employee buyers (even though company money is used versus employee money) do not overpay. This means an independent trustee must be hired to represent the employees to assure a fair price and a that a third-party valuation expert (like a CPA) independently values the business. This value may be less than the owner's expectation and is the number one reason everyone doesn't do an ESOP. You may think the business is worth $20 million, but if the CPA believes it is closer to $10 million, the tax savings may not be enough for the deal to go through.

- Ongoing administration the company must undertake is cumbersome. Among the annual tasks involved, an ESOP requires a business valuation, information requests required from the record keeper (similar to a 401k), coordinated testing needs with other retirement plans, the proper administration of terminated employees, and the management of "repurchase obligation." These are real additional burdens to

ESOP companies and must be considered diligently. Happily, most of these functions can be outsourced, but it will never eliminate the work required, nor all the liability. Note: Employees receive stock to their accounts as a profit sharing allocation. Eventually, when employees leave the company, this stock must be repurchased. Usually, the repurchase is funded as part of the massive tax savings, and the rules spread out the payments over many years, but it must be deliberately managed.

Of course, the tax savings can make up for the lower valuation if valuation expectations aren't too high. It is thus always a good idea to get a valuation before full consideration of an ESOP. Now that I have laid out the major pros and cons of an ESOP, it is important to clarify exactly how ESOPs work. Following are some common misunderstandings of ESOPs:

- **Do employees run the company?** No. The remaining shareholders and/or ESOP trustees run the company depending on who owns 51 percent. ESOP trustees are appointed by the owner, giving the owner control in timing, and, in some cases, they can remain as one of the trustees. Employees only have a "beneficial interest" through their ESOP account, which allows them a vote in limited circumstances (such as a sale to an outside party), but even this vote is limited if ESOP owns less than 50 percent of the stock.
- **Do employees have access to financials?** No, they only receive the business value annually. That being said, numerous studies from NCEO have shown tremendous productivity gains by sharing some financials with employees since they have a stake in the outcome through ESOP stock growth. Companies

like The Great Game of Business help organize selected financials for employees in an organized and fun manner to help boost productivity.

- **Is an ESOP a stock option plan?** No, it is a qualified retirement plan that follows very similar rules to a 401k/profit-sharing plan. The most notable difference is that it is invested in employer stock purchased from a departing shareholder (the BHBO).
- **Do employees use their own money?** No, their interests are built through profit-sharing contributions made to their accounts. The tax savings are helping to fund the buyout to the owner and build wealth for the employees.

If the valuation is reasonable with your expectations, is enough to help you achieve goals from your financial plan, and you have a good team to help, the ESOP can be a fantastic strategy. It is also one of the strategies most likely to help maintain corporate culture and significantly boost the wealth of your long-time employees.

The Family Internal Exit.

Each of the previously discussed tools for internal sales can be used in an exit where a family member is the successor manager of the business, including an ESOP. The biggest difference in the exit of a family business is that you can gift the next generation the business, whereas in a buyout the money is coming from an employee. If you as an owner need more money to fund your goals, gifting may not be a viable strategy. But if you have saved enough outside of the business or have arranged ongoing revenue from the business (such as consulting contracts), gifting may be a great way to minimize estate taxes and keep taxes from wrecking your succession plan.

I discussed several financial planning techniques for reducing transfer taxes in chapter 6, but I held a few aside for this section that are particularly well suited for the transition of a family business. Since a business is typically the largest asset held by a family, its value will frequently push a family past the "unified credit amount" ($24,120,000 for a married couple in 2022) into a taxable estate. Since gifts or bequests over this amount are taxable, the following strategies can help transfer the value of the business to successor family members while minimizing estate taxes.

Family limited partnerships or LLCs. These entities, which are different in each state, have many uses in the context of a family business. They can help manage multiple entities under one umbrella. They can help with asset protection in the event you are sued personally. And they can also help with gifting through a characteristic called "valuation discounts," which are reductions in value for lack of marketability and lack of control. If you had no control and you couldn't sell your business interest, would it be worth as much to you? There have been talks in Congress of limiting this valuation discount. Currently, interests that have these restrictions are not worth as much as having liquidity and control. Limited partnership interests and non-voting interests in an LLC have these restrictions. This creates the ability to make leverage gifts: The underlying holdings of the gift are worth more than the holding itself.

GRIT/GRAT (grantor-retained income/annuity trust). These tools are primarily used to leverage gifts and move future business appreciation to successor owners (called an "estate freeze"). The grantor (you) receives an income or annuity payment for the duration of the trust, after which the trust assets transfer to the beneficiaries. The income received by the grantor offsets the value of the gift, making the taxable gift a lower amount, and all the future appreciation accrues to the next generation. For instance, a $30 million business growing at 10 percent will be worth just under $78 million in 10 years. A GRIT/GRAT can transfer all that appreciation ($48 million) without gift/estate taxes to successor family members if certain conditions are met, potentially saving tens of millions in estate taxes. Additionally, an attorney can make the trust "intentionally defective," which means that you are obligated to pay taxes on business trust income during that term. You must do this because the payment of the taxes is another indirect gift to the successor that is not subject to estate taxes. The downside of these trusts is that the asset moves back into your estate if you pass before the term of the trust.

SCIN (self-canceling installment note). The SCIN is a similar tool as the GRIT/GRAT for an estate freeze, but it is an actual installment note with a self-canceling provision that terminates the note if you were to pass before the end of the term. This carries a risk discount, which reduces the purchase price paid by your successor (or the income from the business). Whereas the GRAT is for longevity, a SCIN is better for estate purposes if you pass before the end of the note since the remaining payments are forgiven for no tax.

External Exits: Higher Valuations, Less Control.

One of the most exciting moments in business is a bidding war to purchase your company, resulting in a consummated business deal. After a deal, investment banks publicize their involvement. Press releases from companies are released. Newspapers cover the transaction. Sellers and buyers are interviewed post transaction on their success. Even popular TV shows such as *Shark Tank* show pitches and deals made between entrepreneurs and investors. Many capital conferences are held across the country promoting deals between entrepreneurs and investors. Do an internet search for "capital conference near me," and you are likely to find an upcoming event. Dozens of books are written on how to pitch to investors, understand the jargon of the investment banking world, and sell your business.

I have seen these deals result in amazing successes and dismal failures. I've seen owners walk away with more money they will ever spend, magnifying their ability to help family and charities. I've seen deals break down with phantom income surprises (taxes you owe without money to pay), friends-coworkers fired and disenfranchised post transaction, cultures wither, and the promised large payouts never happen. Some of the reasons for success/failure are purely business or economy-related and outside of your control. However, the main reason a deal goes sour is that you are uncertain about the goals you wish to achieve. The second most important variable impacting the success of these transactions is finding a serious buyer. The following are the types of buyers and how to choose one:

Financial buyer. A financial buyer is a pool of money (such as a private equity fund) that looks to turn your business into a steady source of income or to be further grown/combined with other similar entities to sell again at a higher multiple. Financial buyers include private equity funds, endowments, family offices, angel funds, or other groups of investors seeking growth or income. "Private equity" is a term for non-publicly traded company ownership and has received much attention in academic and investing circles in the past few years. This positive attention comes from the historically good returns and a reduction of publicly traded companies in the past few years. For today's market, that means there are billions of dollars sloshing around seeking investments making financial buyers competitive alternatives.

If the business is large enough, the company could file for an "initial public offering," which has historically given owners the highest exit multiple. As indicated, fewer companies have been going public in recent years because of the loss of control and intense regulatory scrutiny. Interestingly, special purpose acquisition vehicles (SPACs) have been resurging in popularity to go public with less complication. A SPAC, otherwise known as a "blank check company," is a publicly traded entity that raises money based on the reputation of the managers. The SPAC then goes out with the cash and purchases a business, which becomes a public entity. It can be more straightforward for the selling business as they didn't need to go through the regulatory process of an IPO—they just sell to the already established public entity.

Strategic buyer. A strategic buyer is already involved in a similar type of business and has an interest in yours for a strategic reason. This could be expanding geographic locations, accessing a product line or technology they would find helpful, accessing client lists, or even increasing their manpower by adding your employees. Historically, strategic buyers pay the highest premium on acquisitions, though financial buyers can be aggressive bidders in markets with high liquidity, such as what we saw in 2019.

Criteria to consider. The sale to an outside party most typically involves your continued involvement for a short period (one to three years). This period will include changes to your business as the new owners implement the plan that helps them accomplish their new set of goals. It is important to be comfortable with walking away from the business and understanding that many changes will be made once you are no longer an owner. Of course, a high purchase price can make this far more palatable. So how do you decide whether to choose an external exit for your business? Of course, the goals you spelled out at the beginning of the exit process will be key. If you need the upper end of possible valuation ranges to meet your goals, the external exit may be the best option. If you have more flexibility in this range and/or maintaining some aspect of control in how your business is run after the exit is important to your goals, then another alternative may be better.

Types of Structures

I will discuss more about the types of items needed to negotiate an external exit in the next chapter, but generally speaking, there are four main areas of negotiation as part of a buyout structure:

- **Up-front versus later.** Ideally, a transaction is all cash and immediate, but that is rarely how these deals are structured. The buyer will want you to have some skin in the game to help with the transition and provide "insurance" if it turns out business performance is different from their expectations.
- **Stock versus cash.** Again, cash is better for you, but it is common for a buyer to offer stock in the acquiring company or a "newco" (new company formed to acquire your company) to incentivize a favorable transition. They will sell you as hard on this value as you are selling them on the value of your business.
- **Asset versus stock purchase.** The buyer will be incentivized to purchase your assets versus stock as they can depreciate them in the future (which may trigger depreciation recapture for you). You will prefer a stock sale that is taxed as long-term capital gains.
- **Consulting agreement.** This is the length of time, the outline of accountability, and the compensation you will receive post-transaction. You may end up an employee having to make regular reports to a new boss who can influence the amount of any deferred payment you may have been promised.

Hopefully, this outline gives you some sense that a high purchase price is only one aspect of a good offer, as many items can affect what ends up in your pocket. Following are ways a high purchase price can end up being less attractive:

- A stock purchase where the acquiring stock drops significantly in value
- Stock in a newco where the buyers can trigger phantom income for you (you pay tax on their earnings without a cash distribution)
- Entirely an asset purchase where you pay income versus capital gains taxes on your sale
- A deferred payment triggered by a subsequent sale (sometimes called "second bite") that never happens

Players Needed

In chapter 3, I outlined the importance of having a good team and provided insights on how to choose them. I also mentioned that the team taking you through an exit might be slightly different from the team that helped you build your business. It is entirely possible that your existing team has expertise in these areas or has colleagues who can seamlessly step in to help. The following are a few additional members to consider:

- **Business consultant.** The three years before your business sale will have a massively disproportionate impact on your exit value than any prior year. Hiring a business consultant, especially one with experience preparing for an exit, can help drive the value of your business during these years and prepare the business for sale.
- **Valuation expert.** Some CPAs have valuation certifications, and investment bankers can share comparable business sales to give you a reasonable range of values as you contemplate your options.

- **ESOP expert.** If you pursue this option, you absolutely must hire someone with ESOP experience to avoid the many potential pitfalls.
- **Intermediary.** If you look to sell to an outside party, hiring a business broker or investment banker can be a powerful tool to create a bidding war and drive up the value of your purchase price. In recent years business brokers have been selling larger businesses, and investment bankers have been selling smaller businesses; thus, the differences between the two have been shrinking. Their fees are quite different, but typically you will pay a monthly fee for them to help prepare your business for sale, followed up with a commission on the sale of the business. A great intermediary can be worth their weight in gold as they can help maximize the price of the sale and assist through the closing process to minimize the likelihood a deal falls through. However, the level of industry expertise, contacts in your industry, and sophistication varies widely. Thus, it is imperative you interview several to choose one that is right for your business as it will have a major impact on the eventual value received. We try to work with our clients to identify and hire intermediaries and develop an evaluation spreadsheet available in the resources section of my website to help evaluate alternatives.

Business Documents Organized

In chapter 4 I shared, via my website, a sample due diligence checklist that is typically sent to a seller from a buyer. I also mentioned that the due diligence period is extremely time-consuming. The amount of time required for due diligence is probably the biggest surprise sellers have once they are deep in negotiations after accepting an LOI (letter of intent). It can make your life easier and significantly lessen the disruption to your normal business affairs if you have prepared many of these items prior to an LOI. As I will discuss in the next chapter, this also helps minimize the disruption for employees and helps to keep negotiations private so you don't have questions from employees about what may happen to their jobs post transaction. It may seem like a frivolous project now, but if you're serious about selling your business, make sure your team helps organize your documents prior to embarking on the selling process.

Complete Personal Planning Items

Having already referenced the business owner's financial plan many times in this chapter, it may seem redundant to mention it again, but I want to discuss some of the important items driven by your financial plan that must be completed before a sale to take the most advantage of tax savings. Specifically, if the expected value of your business exit is higher than the amount you need to fund your lifestyle, completing gifting strategies (family and charity) prior to your LOI can save millions in taxes. Did I mention the financial plan is important?

Family Gifting

Gifting before an exit can help reduce income and estate taxes as it can transfer future appreciation and taxes from the sale to the likely lower tax brackets of family members. For instance, let's say you have a business valuation of $30 million that your plan tells you is $10 million more than you need for lifestyle and charitable giving purposes, and you'd like to give your children in a trust. You make those gifts utilizing some of the giving techniques discussed earlier in this book of $8 million (perhaps even retaining rights to income or voting) to ensure you have a little cushion for a potentially lower business exit value. Upon subsequent marketing and sale of the business, you end up selling business for $40 million after focusing on profitability and with the great help of your team. The $8 million gift has appreciated by $2.6 million in their name, avoiding estate taxes potentially over $1 million (not counting taxes saved if you leveraged your gift). Since there are likely to be income taxes paid, and your children are probably in a lower tax bracket, your family will save the difference between their tax bracket and yours. In this example, the savings would be in the six-figure range. Alternatively, if the gift is made *after* the sale, these tax savings are lost.

Charitable Gifting

Similarly, charitable gifts made before a sale can have large tax benefits as a charity will pay no income or capital gains taxes on the sale of your business. Using the same example in the last section, let's say your financial plan allowed for you set up a $5 million gift. With this gift, you would enjoy a $5 million tax deduction (or carry it forward for up to five years, potentially helping to offset other taxes on the sale of your business), and the charity very likely would pay no taxes on the sale of the business. There are exceptions in the case of an S corporation or other types of assets, but proper planning can reduce or eliminate these taxes as well. It is important to know that a charity cannot avoid taxes on UBIT (unrelated business income taxes)—meaning income such as rental income before a sale of a property is taxable. Assuming you started the business from scratch, have a zero-tax basis in your company and the purchase is three quarters capital transaction (capital gains) and one quarter depreciation recapture (income—they purchased the assets from the company before purchasing the stock), then approximately $1.25 million is saved in taxes versus making the gift after the sale. Incorporating ideas from chapter 7 such as the donor-advised fund or a charitable remainder trust, you can design a very powerful plan that helps you reach your income, legacy, and charitable goals. For example, if you weren't sure which charity or charities to support at the time of sale, you could use a donor-advised fund (or your own foundation) to gain the tax advantages at the time of sale but spread out the gifting to charities over many years, all while incorporating these decisions into family discussions. Or, if you do not have kids or have otherwise provided for them and hope to boost your lifetime income, you could use the charitable remainder trust described to reduce capital gains taxes on the sale and boost your income. Possibilities are only limited to your imagination. You, as the owner, need to know what you can afford to give *before* the sale occurs and make that gift before the sale.

Investment Account-Preparing Gate for Your Arrival

While I will discuss managing the proceeds of a business sale in the next chapter, you want to put some deliberate thought into the account that will be receiving a large wire transfer and what you will do in the timeframe between receiving cash and investing. In today's environment of extremely low interest rates, many banking products (money market, checking or savings) may pay close to zero interest rates and may have limited protection from a bank default. $250k FDIC insurance is a very small amount of protection on an account size of $10 million. A good financial advisor can help you with a strategy that reduces risk of principal loss and gives you the opportunity for higher interest rates. The difference on one month's interest from .01% to even a modest rate like .15% on $10 million is $1250 a month. Short term treasury bonds, money market mutual funds investing in high quality securities, a portfolio of short term CDs from various banks, and even specialized bank deposits that spread FDIC insurance over many banks can all potentially combine to increase both the safety and security of your money. If you have had time with your advisor to start working on a long-term investing strategy, your rate of return could obviously be much higher. Ideally, you'll want your money working for you as soon as possible after hitting your account.

❖

In flying, takeoffs do not take tremendous skill unless something goes wrong. I could usually teach a student in one lesson how to safely get into the air. On the other hand, landings require far greater skill and ultimately are a great opportunity for a skilled pilot to show off. I am sure you have judged your pilot on an airline based on the smoothness of your landing. Ninety percent of a good landing is preparation so that the airplane is at the right place, on the correct runway, at the correct airspeed, and in the proper landing configuration. All these things need to be accounted for so a pilot to make a smooth landing. This chapter was all about preparation. The next chapter is making sure it is a smooth touchdown or knowing when to "go around"!

Chapter 9

Landing Smoothly and Enjoying the Destination

**"HAVE I PLAYED MY PART WELL? THEN APPLAUD AS I EXIT."
—AUGUSTUS**

Since landing an airplane is one of the most challenging parts of any flight, the pilot must make many small corrections to assure the wheels touch down safely on the runway. As I mentioned in the last chapter, preparation is the key to a smooth landing, but ultimately the pilot must use their skill to transition from flying to taxiing. When I was a flight instructor, one of the most important tips I taught was to make sure you always keep your eyes down the runway. Once you are in a landing flare, the time for looking inside the cockpit at your configuration is over. You do not want distractions keeping you from making the adjustments necessary to achieve your goal of landing.

The same holds true while you are transitioning through an exit from the letter of intent to the closing table. You want to keep your eyes down the runway, make any adjustments necessary, and keep yourself and your team laser-focused on the reasons for the exit. This won't always be easy as there will be many distractions—such as emotions or surprise findings during due diligence—especially with an external exit.

Once you have followed the advice in this book and landed at your destination, you will have many delightful options. You can become a retired BHBO, or you can start gearing up for your next flight into another business. Just as an airplane follows different rules for control when aerodynamics no longer apply, there is a new set of rules as you transition from running a business to running financial assets. I will also discuss how people pursue happiness in retirement and how to navigate no longer being the boss.

The makeup of a BHBO rarely has them riding off into the sunset, never to be seen again, though you should absolutely enjoy the fruits of your hard labor. More likely, I see the BHBO getting involved in many activities to remain active and continue efforts that are emotionally rewarding to your big heart. I will conclude this chapter with some fun examples.

From LOI to Closing Table: Checklist for Managing Surprises, Problems, and Stress

Here is a useful checklist to help you navigate the sales and closing process. It will help keep you focused during the turbulence that you are likely to encounter during the due diligence process.

Be in touch with your goals, and reference them often. Your goals are the eyes down the runway that you need to keep in mind as the distractions appear. Having them close at hand will help you make good decisions when corrections are required.

Manage employee expectations. Managing employee perceptions and emotions is an important part of the exit process, especially for the BHBO. Each business is different but establishing the timing and narrative of the exit is far better than allowing rumors or the shocking reality of an exit happening to create its own set of issues. Having a communication plan outlining reasons and expectations is critical as you begin the process; then you can decide the timing and groups who receive the message. An external exit also can represent more of a threat of job loss or culture change than an internal exit. I generally recommend that secrecy is maintained until a sale is imminent—especially before potential buyers start touring your facility.

Manage customers. This is a far simpler communication process, but still important. Of course, you have no obligation to say anything. Still, the succession plan of a business can be a very positive story to tell customers: It makes you a more reliable provider of your goods and services. Prepare a strategy and communicate it after the transaction occurs.

Manage family members' expectations. The potential for a liquidity event can create many expectations of family members. You can keep your eyes down the runway by referring to the estate plan you've created.

Manage team members. The most crucial point to remember is that, while team members provide tremendous insights and assistance, you oversee the process. Items found during due diligence can be particularly contentious, and a good attorney will be inclined to fight for every inch. But sometimes, with your eyes on your goals, you need to tell your team to back away.

Manage your expectations, emotions, and stress. The process of negotiation and signing of LOI occurs before the buyer has analyzed every imperfection in your business. Understanding and accepting that due diligence will uncover something unfavorable will help you manage the emotions when it happens. You will also likely be working harder than ever as you try to maintain your business as questions and requests are in full swing. Create your own safe space (time away from everyone) to make decisions and think about the big picture. Do your best to find time for yourself to keep your stress manageable.

You need to keep all stakeholders engaged, but realize you are always in control, even if you don't feel like you are. The process is likely to be one of the busiest and most stressful (yet exciting) times in your life. Knowing generally what to expect and keeping your eyes on your goals through all the crosswinds that will try to push you off the runway will help you grease that landing. Keep your eyes down the runway.

There's a Llama on the Runway!

I've never seen a llama on a runway while landing, but I've seen deer, dogs, cows, and flocks of birds! When the runway is obstructed or otherwise unsafe, you need to go around. Yet, pilots can suffer from an illness known as "get-home-itis." It is a tendency to see what you want to see, ignoring obstacles that may be in your way and risking a good landing (or a good flight) just because you really want to be home. In the context of your exit, the desire to get home can be just as great, but you need to continue to focus on whether the changing conditions will still meet your goals. Most of the time, they will, but sometimes you need to go around.

One of my clients had a tremendous offer from a strategic buyer. It was a mostly cash-upfront deal for an amount that was more than enough to cover his family's goals and greater than he initially expected. Many surprising items came up during the due diligence process: The property was near a superfund site (potential pollution) more than fifty years ago; a large sale was being argued as being non-recurring, thus subtracting from overall profit margins; and the salary of a family member was being questioned. The buyer asked for a slight reduction in the purchase price and for a small additional amount to be put into an escrow and restricted stock (to be unrestricted after three years). The client's attorney also wanted more control over the terms of the escrow account. The deal almost didn't go through because the client's attorney was fighting for each small detail. But even after the changes, the adjusted offer was more than what was expected and more than what was needed, so the client told the attorney to proceed and closed the deal. The site was clean from pollution. Most of the escrow money was paid out. The stock in newco looks promising, and the client is enjoying developing a beautiful family property as they continue to support mission work.

Another one of my clients was approached by a strategic buyer through an intermediary that sought to find out whether my client was interested in a sale. Not being too far from considering an exit, they entertained the bid to test the waters. Initially, the offer and terms were enough to meet goals, but half of the offer price was tied up in stock with the purchasing entity. Due diligence ensued, and nearly every aspect of the deal was challenged early before any site visits. The proposed terms started changing rapidly: the amount of upfront cash, the length the client would need to remain an employee, the escrow amount, and, of course, the ultimate purchase price. It became apparent to my client that goodwill didn't exist to move forward. The client decided to go around and continue to build the business.

Another of my clients with a large business thought an exit may make sense after hearing about high multiples being offered in his type of business. After hiring an investment banker, the young client had several appealing offers on the table. The offer ranges were more than enough to meet the client's financial goals, but his gut had nagging questions: *If they'd offer me this much, could I build the value even higher? What are my aspirational goals?* And the most important question: *What will I do with my time if I sell?* He ultimately decided not to sell because he did not want to be out of the game at his young age. One year later, the 2008 financial crisis hit, and it seemed as if he had made a terrible decision. And perhaps if he were older, it would have been. But he had time to recover. Now the business continues to thrive, and he continues to love working on it as the value has exceeded pre-exploration prices.

While an ESOP is an internal buyer, the initial valuation is a great example of a time for a go/no-go decision. I have seen both expectations of value way below and way above the actual valuation report. Naturally, when the value is below and not enough for goals, it is time for a go-around. If the value is enough, then a landing is possible.

Transitioning from Managing Your Business to Managing Your Financial Assets

Congratulations! You have signed the papers, received the first wire into your account, and received a standing ovation from all the passengers on your landing. You've never seen that many zeroes in your account before.

Now what?

Well, you've certainly earned some time to relax and take a break. Let's pause a moment to consider what that means to you. Vacation? Time at home with family? Staycation? With your money working for you, instead of you working for it (assuming you have an investment strategy established), take your time and smell the roses.

After you return from your break, your brain will start to refocus on the next phase of your life and your financial plan. Invariably, one of the most-asked questions I get from clients with newfound wealth is "How do I understand and manage my financial portfolio better?"

Until now, you've focused most of your time on managing your business (which was the majority of your net worth), and now your net worth has been converted into financial assets, which are part of an investment portfolio. Financial assets are managed differently than a business, but happily many parallels exist, making this transition natural. Stock is ownership in a business. Bonds are loans to a business. You probably managed a real estate portfolio long before your exit. You undoubtedly spent time on cash management within your business. And perhaps you even invested in a few of your friend's business ideas (otherwise called private equity). So be comforted that you are not starting this educational journey from scratch.

Following are some useful guidelines on managing a financial portfolio that will help you understand and evaluate your investment manager and strategies. It is even possible to incorporate some of the values you hold dear as a BHBO into your investment strategies by actively screening your portfolio. Of course, there are few guaranteed rates of return in investing, just like in business. However, a good investing discipline can help dramatically increase the likelihood of success. It's interesting to note that, historically, individual investors have significantly underperformed both institutional investors and the underlying indices they typically own. Why would this be the case? The main reason is that many investors will buy when the markets are rallying and sell when the markets are sinking—the exact opposite of the common advice to buy low and sell high. Among many benefits, discipline can reduce the risk of trying to time the markets unsuccessfully.

Before we get started, I thought it important to share my opinion of the difference between short-term trading and long-term investing to illustrate why I believe the latter is a far more prudent strategy, especially for the high–net worth investor. If you go to a casino, the odds are always stacked in favor of the house. It's possible you can win, and some have had repeated success in gambling, but the fact is that most people lose money. Trading is statistically similar. Each trade has a buyer and seller, a winner and a loser, minus the trading fees taken by the house (commissions, difference between bid and ask prices, or other fees). Long-term investing, on the other hand, has proven time and again to make money far more reliably for those who are patient. If you only purchased the Dow Jones Industrial Average index and held it for ten years or longer, you would make money over 96 percent of the time. Note that's not every single period, but is that not far better than less than 50 percent? Gambling may be fun, but I'd suggest you don't bet your net worth on it. Following are general tips from my training and years of experience that can help slant the odds in your favor.

Learning the Lingo

If you are completely unfamiliar with investing terms, it can be helpful to spend a little time on the internet searching "glossary of investing terms" or "basic investing" on reputable websites. This can help you become familiar with some of the terms, but again recall that the skills of investing and the skills of running a business are related, so be encouraged when you recognize parallels. You can also find hundreds of books about different investment strategies, but this can get quite confusing. I have listed a few investing books and quotes from famous investors on my website that I believe are quite useful and are more aligned with how institutional investors manage money. Several terms I want to define just so you don't get lost:

- **Asset classes:** These are investment holdings that have similar characteristics. Stocks, meaning ownership in a corporation, are an asset class. Bonds, meaning loans to an entity like a company or government, are an asset class. Cash, alternative investments, commodities, and private equity are also examples of asset classes. Finally, each of these asset classes can have subsets; stocks can be international, domestic, large, or small.
- **Asset allocation:** This is the percentage of each asset class that is held in a portfolio. It is the most important factor in the rates of return you will earn in your portfolio. An institutional investor will be deliberate in this asset allocation, whereas many retail investors may randomly select something that looks interesting to them. This deliberate asset allocation can make the difference between investing and gambling. According to a widely cited study, "Determinants of Portfolio Performance," asset allocation will drive 91 percent of your actual performance—far more than security selection, timing, or other factors.

- **Start with your goals:** Here again, goals are important even in managing money! How long before you will need the money? How much is needed to provide your income? Are there other purchases you intend to make? If there are gifts during your lifetime, how much and when? Who are the ultimate beneficiaries? These goals are important to consider, as they give you your time horizon. The longer the time horizon, the more capable your portfolio is of recovering from the ups and downs in the market. It is for this reason that short time horizons should be more conservative than long.

- **Figure out your risk tolerance:** Risk and return are closely related. The more risk you take, the higher the chance of higher returns but also the likelihood you could lose money. In the early example on the ten-year return of the Dow Jones Industrial Average, the index has been up a little more than 73 percent each one-year period. In other words, the longer your time horizon, the more likely riskier holdings are to make money. Some business owners believe they took risks in their business and do not want to risk the portfolio they created. Others believe they should not leave opportunity on the table and want to accept risk. Neither is right or wrong; they simply depend on your risk tolerance. Combined with your time horizon (short will make more conservative and long more aggressive), you now have the baseline amount of risk appropriate for your portfolio. This risk is usually defined as conservative, moderate conservative, moderate, moderately aggressive, or aggressive.

- **Compare to the optimized risk within your financial plan:** Many financial planning software programs will calculate thousands of market scenarios with different portfolios to determine the optimized risk, or the portfolio allocation that gives you the highest probability of success. The industry calls this a Monte Carlo simulation (I don't like the term, as it seems to imply gambling). These programs have many variables: inflation assumed rates of return for asset classes (called capital market assumptions), predetermined asset allocations, taxes, and others. With many variables, it is imperfect and heavily dependent on the expertise of the person using the software. However, a good planner can help you make reasonable assumptions and cross-check your risk tolerance with what the computer says would be optimal. It might change your mind somewhat about the risk you ultimately select. For instance, if you are aggressive but the software believes a moderately conservative portfolio gives you a better chance of success, you might consider the less risky portfolio—or carve off a small portion of a larger, more conservative portfolio to go into a more aggressive strategy.

- **Choose your asset allocation and design an investment policy:** Now you can choose the allocation that best fits your risk profile. Investment firms and managers usually have standard asset allocations for your risk profile that are fairly similar. If you search online for "model asset allocation," you will find dozens of such models. Larger portfolios generally have access to additional investments and asset classes. Thus, we start with an asset allocation targeted toward high–net worth investors, which usually includes allocations to other holdings such as real estate and alternative investments. It is a good idea to formalize this allocation with an investment policy statement, which is a guideline for your manager to stay within your allocation but make small adjustments for tactical ideas. For instance, some managers will become more aggressive or less aggressive based on the shape of the yield curve, which is a curve showing the yield versus how long the bond is held. The yield curve has inverted (short-term yields paying higher than long-term yields) before most recessions. This is not a perfect prediction index, but it can be a tool for tactical adjustments to asset allocation.

- **Diversification within a portfolio:** Harry Markowitz, Nobel Prize winner in economics for his writings on modern portfolio theory, famously said, "Diversification is the only free lunch in finance." While 2008 proved that diversification wasn't a panacea for portfolios since almost everything lost value, diversification is another important investment term, essentially meaning "don't put all your eggs into one basket." Closely related to diversification is the term *correlation*, which is a statistical comparison of whether two investments go up and down in a similar manner. In an ideal world, you could invest in only two holdings with a positive long-term return that is perfectly "noncorrelated," meaning when one goes up, the other goes down, and vice versa. If you remember high school trigonometry, the graphs of sine and cosine show a function that goes up and down. If two investments with a 10 percent return were perfectly noncorrelated, you would get a steady 10 percent return with no fluctuation each year! Unfortunately, no two investments like this exist, but many holdings show a negative correlation with each other, meaning most of the time when one is going down, the other is going up. Choosing a portfolio intentionally for investments that are noncorrelated and with long-term positive rates of return is a way to reduce long-term risk without reducing returns and is the basis for modern portfolio theory and institutional investing. I mention 2008, because assets that normally were noncorrelated (stocks and bonds) became correlated—both lost money. Happily, the markets recovered strongly in 2009, so those investors who maintained their long-term outlook and didn't sell in a panic enjoyed one of the strongest bull market runs in history. Diversification and long-term resolve are powerful investing partners.

- **Choose how you will invest in each asset class:** At its simplest, you could purchase indices of each asset class to fill out your portfolio and be diversified into an appropriate risk profile. Many retirement programs utilize exactly this approach within their balanced or target date portfolios, and many retail investors use these strategies with success. It is difficult for large pools of money to beat the market, so indices can be a great starting point for filling out asset classes. Many examples abound of mutual funds or investing pools starting as small funds that beat the market only to see their performance become closer to that of the index they are trying to beat. Even Warren Buffett has lamented this phenomenon in his letters to shareholders (public information and fantastic reads, highly recommended!) Does this mean opportunities for outperformance do not exist in the markets? I don't believe so. Not only do individual investors frequently make mistakes pushing the market to extremes in either direction (creating opportunities), but there are also sectors of the market too small for the large investors to follow. If you have $5 billion in assets, purchasing a position in a small company will not move the needle. The approach I believe most worthwhile is to use indices when it's difficult to find an actionable opportunity, use managers that are smaller and fly below the radar, and purchase enough positions to diversify without too many positions so you have a higher opportunity to outperform. I will discuss more about this in the next section on high–net worth investing. Past performance is no guarantee of future results. No investing strategy is foolproof. An investment cannot be made directly into an index. The comments are for illustration purposes only and do not predict future performance.

- **Monitor and adjust:** Now that you have chosen an allocation and invested accordingly, it is important to monitor regularly and adjust as appropriate. These adjustments can be tactical— for instance, taking advantage of trends you may see in the market—defensive, if for instance one of your managers has an extended period of underperformance, or periodic rebalancing—which is bringing a portfolio back to its originally intended asset allocation. Several studies have shown the positive impact of rebalancing on long-term performance. For instance, if stocks have had a tremendous run in a conservative portfolio, stocks may have increased from a 30 percent allocation to a 50 percent allocation. Rebalancing helps return that risk to its original level. Though past performance is no guarantee of future success, a March 2020 study by Morningstar Direct compared buy-and-hold portfolios to those annually rebalanced, showing outperformance of the rebalanced portfolios during the 2008 financial crisis, the recession of 2000, and the pandemic of 2020.

Investing Differences as High–Net Worth Investor

How does a portfolio of $1 million or more differ from a smaller portfolio? The three main differences I'll discuss are the ability to purchase your own individual positions in stocks or bonds (versus vehicles like mutual funds); access to alternative investments or non-publicly traded private placements, depending on your financial situation and level of investment experience; and the use of unique risk management tools. All three have the potential to further shape the risk and return of your portfolio in a positive direction.

Purchasing individual positions. Purchasing individual positions can have many benefits over investing through funds or other pooled vehicles. You have a better ability to tax-manage the portfolio, you can write options on positions for risk management, you can craft a bond portfolio specific to the current interest rate environment, you can take advantage of not being too big, and you are not affected by investment decisions that could negatively affect you made by other investors within a common fund.

Tax management: A mutual fund will generally buy or sell positions based on its investment strategy and the number of inflows and outflows from the fund with minimal regard for tax consequences. These funds will flow through their tax consequences to the owners of the fund, meaning you will pay taxes on trades within these funds. Thus, aside from the decision to buy or sell that fund, you have no control over the tax distributions you receive from that fund. With your own portfolio of individual positions, you can choose to hold or liquidate positions yourself with consideration given to taxes. This gives you more tax flexibility plus a higher likelihood that you have a highly appreciated position to gift to a charity (as discussed in chapter 7).

Options writing: Options are complex tools that can help change the risk or income profile of your portfolio more to your objectives. As a brief primer, options (which consists of puts and calls) are derivatives of an underlying position such as a stock or exchange-traded fund—meaning their prices are dependent on the prices of the underlying position. Why can they be useful? Options allow a manager to further shape the risk/return profile of that underlying position: either increasing or decreasing the risk and increasing or decreasing the yield on that position. Using options to increase risk is not a strategy we typically employ in our practice, so I do not have many insights. However, we find using options to increase yield or decrease risk can be a useful way to help shape portfolios' risk/yield characteristics more in line with investment objectives. As in everything, there are always tradeoffs. For instance, increasing yield may result in giving up gains in a rapidly rising market. If you want more details, you can access a good pamphlet from Options Clearing Corporation (www.theocc.com/ Company-Information/Documents-and-Archives/ Options-Disclosure-Document). (Note: This site is shared for informational purposes only and is not an offer of investment advice or options trades.)

Bond management: Owning individual bonds versus a fund can allow numerous potential investing advantages. You can choose to hold bonds to maturity to reduce the negative impact of a rising rate environment; you can match bond maturities with your personal cash needs; and your portfolio is unaffected by the buying or selling of other investors within a fund. Again, this gives you more control over your portfolio. When interest rates are rising, the value of bonds typically drops. It makes sense if you think about it: If I bought a five-year bond paying 1.5 percent and then interest rates go up to 2 percent, nobody wants my 1.5 percent bond, so I'd have to sell it for less. But if I hold it to maturity, I get all my money back from a solvent issuer. Of course, falling rates increase bond prices. If interest rates drop to 1 percent, my 1.5 percent bond looks great, and I could sell at a premium. Bonds have been on a bull market run ever since the 1970s, when interest rates were in the double digits. If interest rates resume/continue an upward climb and hurt bond portfolios, will fund investors sell? If you hold a fund and other investors are rapidly selling that fund, the manager must sell bond holdings to pay those investors. It's entirely possible the manager would sell at a bad time and take a loss, which could hurt your returns even though you were holding on. A portfolio of individual bonds does not have this risk of your performance being impacted by other fund shareholders.

Creating your own portfolio versus joining a large pool: Certainly, large pools of money have advantages, such as usually lower transaction costs. However, as discussed earlier with the example of Berkshire Hathaway, being a "smaller" portfolio also has some significant advantages. While there certainly are exceptions, much has been written about the difficulty of some funds replicating early success once they have grown to several billion in assets under management. Many funds limit their size and shut out new investors to try to protect their performance.

This makes sense if you think about it, especially for funds focusing on stocks in small companies. If I'm a fund manager focusing on small publicly traded companies, my portfolio performs well, and investors start putting a good deal of money into my fund, I may have too much money to invest in small companies. For instance, if my fund grew from $100 million (where a $5 million investment would be 5 percent of my fund) to $1 billion (where $50 million is now 5 percent of my fund), my $50 million might be larger than the entire company I'm looking to purchase.

So how many stocks are ideal within a portfolio? Five? Twenty? A hundred? There is the risk that one company has horrible performance and takes down an entire portfolio, called unsystematic risk. Generally speaking, you can reduce most of this risk by holding more than twenty positions. Other studies look to an ideal number of stocks that could outperform an index. Again, there are many exceptions to this rule, but some research indicates that having a portfolio of twenty to fifty stocks rather than several hundred gives the investor a higher likelihood of returns that beat the index. Naturally, no strategy is guaranteed to work every time, but it helps put the odds in your favor.

Access to alternative investments. First, what are alternative investments, or AI? Generally speaking, AI is any investment outside of stocks, bonds, or cash. Accordingly, it is an extremely broad category, comprising commodities, cryptocurrencies, futures, private equity, real estate, and a large array of hedge funds with different esoteric strategies (global macro, long/short, market-neutral, merger arbitrage, to name a few). The common theme of most of these strategies is that regulators require minimal income or assets to qualify for these holdings. Since there are so many types, you can imagine each has its own risk/return profile, with some being extremely aggressive and some being very conservative. Why include it in a portfolio? The main reason has been that many AI assets are highly non-correlated (remember from earlier, they zig when other assets

Cryptocurrencies as an asset class. Cryptocurrencies (crypto for short) are a relatively new asset in finance based on "blockchain" technology. They have created an entirely new ecosystem called decentralized finance ("defi," for short), with blockchain being one of the most rapidly adopted new technologies in history. We have been keenly interested in investment opportunities within public and private companies that apply blockchain to the new or disruptive use of the exciting technology.

But what about the opportunities to invest directly into cryptocurrencies like Bitcoin or Ethereum? From a purely statistical standpoint, crypto has the characteristics of a good asset class for diversification: It has a very competitive historical rate of return, and it has a low correlation with equity markets. The anonymous founder of Bitcoin (pseudonym Satoshi Nakamoto) created it as the first *public* ledger intending to be an alternative currency outside the hands of centralized banks and governments. As of now, regulatory agencies in the United States and other countries are still figuring out how to treat it for tax and regulatory purposes. Some, like El Salvador, have adopted it as their currency. Other governments, zag) and have historically very competitive returns. Alternative investments gathered much attention after tremendous success within the endowment world, specifically the Yale Endowment under the late Dr. David Swensen. Going to their website and looking at their returns and asset allocation can be an illuminating experience; for instance, nearly 40 percent of the fund is invested in venture capital and leveraged buyouts as of 2020. Dr. Swensen was also among the first to caution against exact replication of his strategies since Yale has access to some exclusive hedge fund arrangements. However, the returns on private equity can be quite compelling—perhaps you even sold to a private equity firm! The world of alternatives and private placements is very complicated and regulated and usually has high fees, so be sure to understand the criteria before you invest.

including Switzerland, are looking to create their own cryptocurrencies. Some countries (China, for one) have even banned them.

With thousands of different cryptocurrencies now in circulation, this is a rapidly changing area full of opportunities and pitfalls. Which ones will remain in five years? Will governments seize or ban their use, hurting their value? Will evolving technologies prove capable of the volumes needed to truly provide an alternative currency? Will some cryptos become a more stable source of value without the large fluctuations we've seen in larger ones like Bitcoin?

These answers are currently unknowable, but I believe crypto is here to stay. As I mentioned, the argument for crypto as a valuable asset class is quite compelling, as long as investors understand it also has the high potential to "go to zero," for instance if the one you choose proves obsolete compared to others or if governments ban their use. Of course, companies can go bankrupt, too. Risk is always inherent in investing. But the risk/reward of crypto is clearly very high. I believe it is an asset worth consideration if investors understand the high risks inherent in the asset class.

The alternatives may include hedge funds or even investing directly into opportunities that are presented to you (such as a local business). Some of these options can be quite appealing for the savvy investor, but they are usually quite risky. Do your research if you so choose to pursue it.

Use of unique risk management tools. Business owners are accustomed to taking risks, but I find that most are more conservative with their investment portfolios. These individuals are often older once they have seen an exit, and the portfolio represents a lifetime's worth of work. Of course, there is risk in everything, even cash (inflation). But a good manager can help reduce these risks with a few strategies built into portfolios:

> **Options:** As discussed earlier, options are tools used to modify the risk structure of stocks or ETFs. They are sometimes called derivatives since their entire value is based on those underlying positions. The money you receive or pay is called a premium. You pay a premium to purchase one or receive a premium if you sell one. A **put** is an option that will gain in value when the value of the position drops, making them suitable for reducing the risk of an underlying position. A **call** is an option that will gain when the value of the position gains. It gets complicated because you can take long or short positions in options. One of the more conservative strategies is covered call writing, which involves giving up potential appreciation in return for higher current income. It works well in a slowly rising market, but you can miss opportunities in a rapidly rising market. Protective puts are another strategy, essentially buying insurance on your portfolio. They can limit losses in down markets, but sometimes the premium you pay is expensive. An experienced

advisor can help assist you in understanding your options and make sure you read the options document referenced earlier.

Structured products: As you might suspect, a large institution can buy or sell large blocks of options for a lower overall cost than individual investors can. Accordingly, many institutions will create structured products that utilize their purchasing power to structure an investment product with a set of risk/return characteristics that they believe will appeal to investors. High-net-worth investors can even partner with a financial institution to design a product specifically for them. These products usually exchange liquidity (they typically have a term of several years) for potentially higher rates of return with lower levels of risk. The structure of them can get quite complicated. But for those with ample cash or other liquid holdings, this can be a useful tradeoff that has the potential to increase returns without increasing risk. For instance, I have seen some structured CDs with full FDIC protection track the S&P 500 or Eurostox 50 indices for potential market returns, with just four- to six-year holding periods. With no risk of loss, the main risk is opportunity cost—not being able to invest in something else.

Additionally, you could pledge these positions to banks in return for a security-based line of credit to maintain some liquidity if it is needed. (Note: Such loans cannot be used to purchase other securities.) This can provide a useful combination of liquidity and competitive returns. Structured products are generally issued as either bonds by the institution (subject to solvency risk of that issuer) or as CDs, which carry

FDIC insurance up to their limits. Because of the conservative nature of these positions, security-based lines of credit can have high loans to value—in CDs, typically 90 percent of the value. Structured notes typically have more competitive terms than CDs since they carry more risk.

Annuities: The annuity industry has seen dramatic improvements in its design through the years. Initially designed simply to provide guaranteed lifetime income and some tax deferral, newer products have features that can accomplish many more goals. The growth of an annuity can be based on a minimum guaranteed rate of return, mutual funds, or indices. They can include multiple riders, such as those that protect account value, those that protect income, those that provide long-term care costs, or those that protect beneficiaries. While complicated, annuities can also be a useful tool for creating a less risky stream of income that can last for a lifetime while also carrying some tax-deferral and asset protection depending on the state where you live.

Behavioral finance. We humans do silly things. We are overly influenced by fear and greed. To simplify massive amounts of information, we pay attention to things that either give us a distorted vision of reality or distract us from more important items. The study of how the human element distorts trading and financial markets is called behavioral finance. In my opinion, this is the area with the biggest difference between when you ran your business and now running a financial portfolio. The markets can be manic, with price swings sometimes not based on fundamentals. I doubt wild market fluctuations had a huge impact on your opinion on the value of your business. Yet, poor decisions happen in public markets regularly because of two very powerful human emotions—fear and greed—coupled with our instincts to follow the herd. One of my favorite Benjamin Graham quotes illustrates this point: "In the short run, the market is a voting machine. In the long run, it's a weighing machine." The public markets are the collective voting machine of millions of investors who buy and sell positions rapidly and not always rationally. An internet search for "behavioral finance" will turn up many ways individual investors have let their emotions get the better of them. I will start by saying that the best solution for all these biases is having a discipline and sticking to that discipline as markets get volatile. Spock would have been a great investor; try to invest like him and separate your emotions from your investment decision-making. Following are a few examples of how our emotions can negatively affect our investment decisions:

Self-serving bias. In a 2018 American Automobile Association poll, over 70 percent of respondents said they were above-average drivers. Obviously, this cannot be true. Similarly, many investors will attribute gains to their skill and losses to bad luck. One of my favorite investing books is *Fooled by Randomness* by Nicolas Taleb. Among the brilliant points is the observation that it can be quite difficult to differentiate luck from skill in the financial markets. This can be avoided by identifying what is statistically replicable and not making decisions on a gut feeling.

Fear and greed. Generally, the fear of loss is stronger than the greed for gain. However, both lead to imperfect decision-making. Morningstar tracks both the performance of funds and the performance of investors within those funds, and the difference is staggering. In some cases, investors are earning barely more than half the returns of the underlying funds. This is because investors are simply buying and selling at the wrong times: buying high and selling low. Unfortunately, investors have a habit of putting more money into the markets during bull markets than bear markets, leading to under-performance. One of a financial advisor's greatest values is helping investors make rational decisions when the markets are overcome with fear and greed.

Anchoring. Anchoring is picking an easy-to-remember number and then making decisions based on that number. For instance, once an account reaches a round number (like $1 million), it is common to become more afraid and sensitive to loss once it has passed through that milestone. Some may anchor to an initial account value, treating gains as house money and therefore becoming more aggressive with money that has been earned. Decisions instead should be based on the risk tolerance, time horizon, and goals rather than the anchored number.

Institutions historically have outperformed retail investors by doing a better job of understanding their discipline and following it through different market environments. If they know they will be buying in certain bear markets, it will be easier for them to follow through when the bear market occurs. If they know they will be selling when a stock reaches a certain level, it will again be easier to do when it reaches that point. The best solution to overcoming these biases is having discipline and sticking to that discipline as markets get volatile.

Incorporating Your True North into Investing Processes

Selling your business changes the structure of your balance sheet, but it does not change your true north. This section will explore ways to incorporate your values into how you invest.

- **ESG and the BHBO.** As I mentioned in chapter 5, ESG stands for environmental, social, and governance investing and is a relatively new investing style sometimes called "impact investing" or SRI: socially responsible investing. While you can incorporate these values into your business, you can also incorporate them into your investing style. ESG has seen tremendous growth in recent years. According to the 2021 Sustainable Funds Landscape Report by Morningstar, fund flows increased from 1 percent in 2014 to 25 percent in 2020. ESG investing involves a screen of stock or bond holdings for certain ESG characteristics in the hope that those investments both perform better than without the screen and align their true north with their portfolio. For instance, screening out companies with a more negative impact on the environment through pollution or carbon emissions can be one of many screens. Is this perfect for the BHBO? Well it depends on if ESG screens match your values and whether those screens keep out underperforming holdings. A quick internet search will show that ESG has performed well the last few years, though some would argue that the outperformance is primarily due to an overweight of tech companies (that have outperformed the market) while screening out energy companies (that have underperformed). Being a new investing style, the verdict is still out on whether such screens give investors significant performance advantages, but some studies have shown promise. For instance, much has been written about companies performing better that have women on their boards, even if other studies have argued little difference in performance. However, these screens can certainly help you align your true north with your portfolio. At first blush, it may seem that ESG is a way to align politics with investing—and indeed, it could be if taken to the extreme. However, I have known many conservative investors who have expressed an interest in ESG once they gain a greater understanding of the screens, which can be appealing to all political stripes. For instance, some new ESG funds are focusing on Christian values. Environmentally friendly companies that take care of their employees and have good governance are not necessarily red or blue. Notably, more companies like Morningstar are analyzing ESG characteristics for investors to consider, and more publicly traded companies are providing ever-increasing transparency on ESG criteria. However, it is important to note that the standards are still not universal even as some organizations (like SASB—Sustainability Accounting Standards Board) are trying to bring uniformity. Following are more details on the types of screens available to the investor:

- ○ **Environment screens:** These are screens based on the negative environmental impact of a company (carbon or other emissions). Since most companies have some environmental impact, the standards to pass or fail a screen are currently still developing. Thus, it's important to understand whether the screen you choose is consistent with your true north. Many corporations have formed sustainability departments to help analyze their environmental footprint and be more deliberate in their efforts to curb negative environmental impact. Even some companies that traditionally have failed this screen (like energy) are working toward sustainability and less environmental impact.

- ○ **Social screens:** Social screens are measures of how a business interacts with employees, business partnerships, and the community. Taking care of others is quite a broad term. A social screen can include the strength of benefits, the overall compensation of employees, sometimes employee satisfaction, working conditions, and sometimes can include diversity measures. It is also becoming more common to include how the company treats suppliers/other business relationships and how the company may contribute to the local community and/or encourage charitable employee activities. This is one of the largest areas of evolution within publicly traded companies and includes many opportunities for the BHBO to align with their true north.

- **Corporate Social Responsibility (CSR) Departments:** It is becoming more common to see larger private and publicly traded companies with departments dedicated to these areas—not just to placate ESG investors but also to provide a more positive workplace environment and align corporate activities with corporate values. These offices can focus on diversity/inclusion, charitable activity within a community, encouraging or tracking charitable volunteer work by employees, making charitable donations, encouraging employee donations, and so on. Indeed, even a new tech start-up sector is being built around charitable tech to help make the promotion of these values easier.
- **Governance screens:** Governance is the process behind how a company makes important decisions. These screens include transparency of accounting; the constitution, experience, and power of a board; the relationship between management and the board; and the potential conflicts of interest of decision-makers. The accounting profession had studied this area long before ESG emerged. As such, governance is likely the easiest to track of all screens, which do have more universal standards.

Ultimately, you will need to decide whether to add these types of screens to your portfolios. The resources to provide investors with useful information on ESG are increasing by the day: Corporations are being more deliberate about their own ESG goals; companies like Morningstar are providing tools for ESG screening of stocks, bonds, and mutual funds with ESG objectives; and investors are being more aware of this investing discipline.

Planning Your Next Flight: New Business Ventures

Upon your well-earned retirement, your next flight might be to the beach or the pool. Some BHBOs, however, are still young and have the desire and the energy to start another business. If this is you, the experience of having been through the business cycle from start-up to exit can be a great advantage in starting another company, as you have already made mistakes you don't care to repeat. Additionally, finding capital may be a little easier since you probably have a healthier balance sheet of your own, and banks and investors are more likely to lend or invest with someone who has a proven track record. However, it is important to remember that even being an experienced entrepreneur does not guarantee success in your next business. Be sure you do not waste all the financial success from your first business. What are some considerations for beginning another flight?

Know how much of your balance sheet you are willing to again put at risk. Here, again, referencing the business owner's financial plan is an important starting point. You can set aside the money you want to protect your lifestyle (and reassure family) while determining the amount you feel comfortable losing if the next venture does not go as planned.

What are the goals for the next venture? Is it to continually build your balance sheet? Is it to keep your mind active and stay in the game? Knowing yourself will help you stay centered on the next flight that you will find rewarding.

Does your spouse support the idea of a new venture? What does your family think of the idea? What would the conditions be to keep your family happy? Another way a BHBO can stay involved in the business without putting their lifestyle at risk is by mentoring other business owners. I've seen numerous rewarding ways entrepreneurs who have exited their businesses have made a huge positive impact on their business community—some of which I mentioned earlier in the book as sources of capital.

Local accelerators: Many communities have for-profit, non-profit, or local government-funded accelerators designed to support the new business owner and increase their chance of success. They usually help through mentorship, resources (shared space, coding, collaboration), introductions to potential business partners, and connections to capital. Most benefit greatly from owners willing to share their time and talent. This allows the BHBO to stay involved in business with less time commitment, and potentially invest in promising businesses or people. Ask your local advisors about what is available in your area.

SCORE: Service Corps of Retired Executives is a program run by the SBA to provide resources to small business owners with the help of (you guessed it!) retired BHBOs who hope to assist. They also help with SBA funding when appropriate for the new business. With nearly 400 locations, you'll likely find one near you or visit www.score.org.

Tech transfer offices or business courses at universities: Many universities have developmental offices designed to help students or professors turn a discovery or idea into a commercial success. Depending on your expertise and the sectors supported at your local university, you could be a quite useful and fascinating resource for them. I have also seen many a BHBO assist with teaching business courses at local schools.

Angel investing groups: Part social networking, part private equity, many communities also have angel groups that organize pitches by local entrepreneurs, allow members to assist in funding, help support the entrepreneur through mentorship, and track the business's ongoing success. You will find much online with a search for "angel investing" in your community. Of course, these are risky investments, but they can have other rewards besides the potential for monetary gains.

Mission work: A mission doesn't necessarily need to be far away, nor does it need to be focused only on helping to build physical structures, such as schools or homes. I have seen several of my clients help establish business support infrastructures in rural communities to assist and train people in entrepreneurship. I've seen these types of efforts work well locally with youth entrepreneur centers, regionally with areas lacking resources, and internationally with missions all intending to "teach a man (or woman) to fish" versus feeding them one meal. My sister even spent a year in Senegal with the Peace Corps helping locals establish start-up businesses. There is also a fascinating area called microfinancing, which helps inject capital into poor areas internationally. An internet search can open up a world of information on these new and exciting areas of finance.

Enjoying the Destination (Retirement) as a BHBO

You have "taken it to the house!" Even though it may seem daunting to have freed up so much time, you will likely find that you fill it up rather quickly! Most will wonder how they ever had time to go to work. Hopefully, your financial plan was specific enough to know the types of activities and ventures you will pursue during retirement. Perhaps it's travel, building a vacation home, spending time with family, spending more time on your hobbies, appreciating beauty, mission trips, or more involvement with your charitable causes. Everyone's ideal retirement is unique to them, but some characteristics of retirement remain constant. A great study by MIT AgeLabs (www.agelab. mit.edu) attempted to link these constant types of activities with a high quality of life and simplified it into three questions: Who will change my lightbulbs? How will I get an ice cream cone? Who will I have lunch with? I'd highly recommend reading the study online. The study discusses interesting ideas important to retirees, including housing, travel and mobility, and social connection. For instance, it shares some of the latest information on smart homes, which incorporate technology into the ease of managing a residence.

It can be helpful to explore other resources through retirement to generate ideas on having a fulfilling retirement, which could be thirty years or more. With improvements in medicine, people who are in their sixties today can expect to live into their nineties! Think of all you accomplished in thirty years and realize much can happen and change in this phase of life. The AARP, state offices on aging, longevity resources from your financial advisor, and churches can be great sources of ideas and information. These resources can provide insights on topics such as long-term care, travel resources, and managing health care costs.

Of course, none of these issues address the inevitable questions we ask as we become more contemplative about our lives while getting closer to sunset. It can be easier to feel more alive when cheating death in our youth, but what about feeling more alive as our bodies tell us otherwise? How do we truly know that we have made a difference and that we've had lives worth living? Such questions are an inherent part of the BHBO and core to their true north. While I mentioned "beginning with the end in mind" in chapter 1, it feels a little different when fewer pages remain in the story of our lives. It can be inspiring to explore these topics with groups, readings, or people who light up your thoughts. I've been blessed to have several people close to me write books or articles on such questions and feel unbelievably fortunate to have gained from their wisdom. Retired minister and ethics professor

Dr. Bert Keller and his friend and family physician, Dr. Jim Simpson, write a column in my local paper, *The Charleston Post and Courier*, titled "Aging for Amateurs." Simpson discusses the health aspects of aging, including healthy tips, while Keller discusses the spiritual and emotional aspects of aging, also embedded with nuggets of wisdom. Among the many focuses of retirement introspection, I believe gratitude is one of the most important.

The beauty of gratitude is that it can be found everywhere, all the time, if you're looking. Living a grateful life during each stage of the journey is a common characteristic of the BHBO. Indeed, gratitude for an amazing journey, a life well loved, friends and family, precious memories, and all the little things give in us that feeling of abundance, give us the power to inspire, and ultimately give us power to give of ourselves. "His Lord said unto him, Well done good and faithful servant; thou hast been faithful over a few things, I will make thee ruler over many things: enter thou into the joy of thy Lord." —Matthew 25:23.

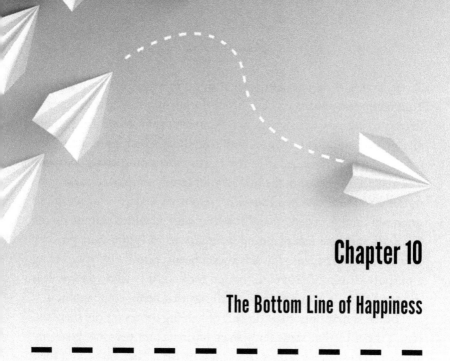

Chapter 10

The Bottom Line of Happiness

"A WISE MAN SHOULD HAVE MONEY IN HIS
HEAD, BUT NOT IN HIS HEART."
–JONATHAN SWIFT

We've taken quite a journey together exploring *The Bottom Line of Happiness*. We have set our compass with specific intentions and planned for our trip. We have chosen the right people to join our team and used the best instruments to navigate safely as guided by our true north. We have learned about the plane we're flying, adjusted our course when things went wrong or the skies grew stormy, and have landed smoothly at our destination. We have even discussed how to successfully settle into this important new phase of your life. Congratulations on your successful flight!

For some business owners, this new, more carefree phase of life is all about relaxing, traveling, and celebrating success. Hopefully, you will do plenty of that, too. But as a BHBO, your focus has always been about serving the bigger purpose of your life, whatever that might be. Your happiness has always come from the pursuit of something greater than your business achievements and monetary successes. Throughout all the ups and downs of your often tumultuous journey as a business owner, you have never stopped striving to grow a prosperous company *and* make a difference in the lives of your family, employees, and community. You have donated your time, resources, and growing wealth to nonprofits and heartfelt causes. You have worked with a team to do the financial and business planning necessary to integrate your purpose into the journey because this has always been a priority for you. Living a purpose-driven life is not an option for you. It is who you are. It is in your DNA. It is one of the core things that bring you happiness.

BHBOs never put their dreams of helping others on the shelf and say, "I'll get to that someday." Their business and personal goals are aligned from their early days as business owners. They care about their families, their people, and their community. They are good neighbors. That's why they give of themselves *while* they are building amazing, successful companies. Though many BHBOs are too humble to admit it, they have already made the world a better place and shaped a meaningful legacy for themselves well before landing at their destination in retirement. The world is a better place because of them.

As author Farrah Gray has said, "Money doesn't change who you are; it magnifies who you really are." That's how you should see money and success: as an opportunity to augment the good work you have been doing your whole life. Your business-building days might be over, but your work is not done, because that's not who you are. Yes, after all those years of juggling competing priorities, putting out fires, and driving the growth of your company, you have left the daily grind. But now, finally, you have time to fully embrace your passion projects. As a result, this new phase of your life will be filled with the happiness you have always experienced when immersed in service to your life's purpose. To paraphrase the words of American speaker and social reformer Henry Ward Beecher, you are rich because of who you are, not what you have.

Unfortunately, many business owners don't feel these types of positive emotions when they enter retirement. In fact, they often feel lost. As a result, many suffer from depression. As a January 28, 2021, article on the topic in verywellmind.com stated one reason for post-retirement depression is that "the person's sense of self is tied up very strongly in what he or she does for a living; and, with retirement, a sense of loss can occur, leaving a person struggling to understand who they are and what their value is." Allow me to slightly reinterpret the words of American business author Gretchen Rubin: Money and success are good servants, but bad masters. If you are feeling afraid to retire or lost in your retirement, it is never too late to find your purpose in life. Look around. There are so many organizations that could benefit from your skills. Many of them are probably only a short drive from your house. Reach out and start volunteering. It will shift everything—your perspective and your life.

Luckily, as a BHBO, this is not a challenge you are likely to face. Because of your purpose-driven approach to work and life, you have not identified your personal worth too closely with your business. As a result, you don't feel empty and unmoored after selling it off and retiring. Quite the opposite. Though the schedule and lifestyle transition to retirement can be dramatic and jarring, your life is a continuum. Your business and personal goals have been aligned for a long time. You've always had the big picture in mind, and that picture is bigger than your company. Meaning has always been more important to you than money. But you are wise enough to know that money, if used intentionally, can support you on your mission. That's why your purpose is the thread that weaves all the diverse aspects of your business and personal life together into a single, amazing, colorful tapestry.

Saint Francis of Assisi said that it is in giving that we receive. Well, you have been giving your whole life and now you are receiving one of the many gifts of a well-planned BHBO retirement: There's plenty of time and money for you to do many more years of meaningful work because of your past planning to reach your destination. You'll be reaping the benefits of those efforts for the rest of your life, as will the people and organizations you plan to help. Guided by your unique values, ethics, passions, and deeply held beliefs, you have successfully maximized your business in a way that will now allow you to maximize your time, money, and talents for the highly meaningful work ahead. Your journey is far from over, and you have made sure that the tailwinds are favorable for the rest of your journey.

Throughout my career, I have had the distinct honor of working as a financial advisor with many amazing BHBOs. Working with this type of client is a sweet spot in my financial practice. I'm passionate about helping these good people do good things with the best vehicles to build and exit from their great companies. As a BHBO myself, it is very gratifying work. I love my job and the clients I serve. That is part of *my* purpose in life. However, when I started writing this book and told people the title would be *The Bottom Line of Happiness*, inevitably, I heard from friends, "Matt, you know you can't buy happiness." They were mostly teasing, but I wanted to address this idea that happiness can't be bought. It's true, to an extent, but quite misleading.

I believe—having witnessed positive outcomes for decades—that with good financial planning, alignment of personal and professional goals, the right financial instruments and planning team, and a strong sense of purpose, you can do more of what you love, help more people, and ultimately experience the joy that comes from these meaningful experiences. There is research to support this idea. Here's an overview from a February 7, 2021, article in *Forbes* titled "New Study Shows That More Money Buys More Happiness, Even for The Rich." The article gives a great overview of the last decade's worth of research on this topic:

> In 2010, psychologist Daniel Kahneman and economist Angus Deaton (who both won the Nobel prize in Economics) undertook research to ascertain if money played a part in two aspects of people's emotional lives. Firstly, the everyday quality of daily life, the joy, stress, sadness, anger, and affection that make one's life pleasant or unpleasant. And secondly, life

evaluation—the thoughts that people have when they think about their lives.

The study found that money did have an impact for how people evaluate their lives when they think about it; that people with more money feel better about their lives. However, emotional well-being rose with income, as expected too, but only to an annual salary of $75,000 ($90,000 in today's money). Beyond that, people were no happier with higher salaries. The seminal study concluded that whilst "low income is associated both with low life evaluation and low emotional well-being," ironically, "high income buys life satisfaction but not happiness."

Matthew Killingsworth is now a senior fellow at the University of Pennsylvania's Wharton School and has a history of tracking happiness–he even created a tool for it. Track Your Happiness is an application that investigates what makes life worth living. Killingsworth was developing the app, according to Bloomberg, around the same time as Kahneman and Deaton were doing the research for the 2010 study.

The idea is you tell the app what you are feeling at several points throughout the month, thereby contributing to Killingsworth's scientific experiment but also helping the user find out what factors are associated with their greater happiness. As the app says, the world's greatest thinkers have always agreed that happiness is a core life goal but "enormous improvements in human life–bigger houses, more powerful technology, better medical care–have achieved only modest improvements in happiness."

The conclusion to Killingsworth's research has just been published in *Proceedings of the National Academy of Sciences*. By tracking reported happiness in relation to reported income, the study found that—like the 2010 research—both life satisfaction and experienced well-being increased with income. However, unlike the 2010 research, well-being continued to increase as steeply past an annual income of $80,000 as it did below it. The conclusion, therefore, is "that higher incomes may still have potential to improve people's day-to-day well-being, rather than having already reached a plateau for many people in wealthy countries."

What I find most interesting in this article, and the research it covers, is in the second-to-last paragraph. Here, the author of the article, Alex Ledsom, reports that the app's advice, based on the wisdom of the ages, is not to pursue the accumulation of things, as it will only help achieve modest improvements in happiness. More hopeful is that last paragraph, which I believe contains data that hints at a changing world in which more people are using their money to support meaningful living rather than the accumulation of more things. Perhaps in these numbers, we are seeing more BHBOs as I see them in my own practice. Gratitude is a trait the BHBO has regardless of wealth. However, I believe wealth magnifies this feeling of gratitude and the motivation to give back. While some causes of the BHBO don't show up on a tax return (like taking care of family), I do see firsthand charitable giving increase more than proportionately in reviewing the tax returns of clients as their income grows. Indeed, Giving Tuesday Data Commons found that in 2020, during a global pandemic, the total amount of all charitable donations came from gifts made of over $50,000, having more than doubled over 2019! This was in a timeframe where the total number of gifts over $50,000 remained about the same; those who had the means were simply more generous. And in another positive sign, the total number of donations of $100 to $500 increased the most. Despite the vitriol shown on the news, people were quite generous.

There are other signs of this trend. The "purpose economy" is a term coined by Aaron Hurst in 2014 in a book with the same title. In the book, Hurst describes the emergence of a new type of economy that "fosters the flow of good ideas, the creation of positive and impactful service, and ultimately a more efficient way to spread good in the world." Hurst predicted that the purpose economy would come of age in 2020, and he has data to back up his claim. As consumers, we're seeing this shift all around us. Companies like Patagonia, TOMS, Bombas Socks, Miir, Warby Parker, and many others are leading the way. These companies are shifting the way we make purchase decisions for the better.

But I think that deep down most of us know that buying more things won't buy us more happiness, even though all too often we are dazzled by the quick gratification of consumerism. Dr. Thomas Gilovich, a psychology professor at Cornell University, has been studying the question of money and happiness for more than two decades. In an April 30, 2015, *Fast Company* article titled "The Science of Why You Should Spend Your Money on Experiences, Not Things," Dr. Gilovich told journalist Jay Cassano, "We buy things to make us happy, and we succeed. But only for a while. New things excite us at first, but then we adapt to them." The article went on to explore Dr. Gilovich's findings in more depth:

> Gilovich's findings are the synthesis of psychological studies conducted by him and others into the Easterlin Paradox, which found that money buys happiness, but only up to a point. How adaptation affects happiness, for instance, was measured in a study that asked people to self-report their happiness with major material and experiential purchases. Initially, their happiness with those purchases was ranked about the same. But over time, people's satisfaction with the things they bought went down, whereas their satisfaction with experiences they spent money on went up.
>
> It's counterintuitive that something like a physical object that you can keep for a long time doesn't keep you as happy as long as a once-and-done experience does. Ironically, the fact that a material thing is ever present works against it, making it easier to adapt to. It fades into the background and becomes part of the new normal. But while the happiness from material purchases diminishes over time, experiences become an ingrained part of our identity.

"Our experiences are a bigger part of ourselves than our material goods," says Gilovich. "You can really like your material stuff. You can even think that part of your identity is connected to those things, but nonetheless they remain separate from you. In contrast, your experiences really are part of you. We are the sum total of our experiences."

To me these findings are just another sign that people are moving toward more meaningful, purpose-driven activities in their lives and money is simply the vehicle to find and fuel them. Working with so many BHBOs in my line of work, I get to see what that kind of life looks like all the time. And I can tell you, what I have the privilege of seeing are very rich and fulfilling lives that are infused with happiness and gratitude.

These owners have certainly inspired me to mirror them in my own life. I've discovered my true north from a combination of my Christian faith and my martial arts background, which keeps me in touch with my mortality. I consider myself a quiet evangelist—as a Christian, I've always felt it most comfortable to be as good an example as I can be: "known by my love." As Jesus loving the little children has always resonated, my life has been dedicated to helping underprivileged youth. I was a Big Brother when I was earning less than $12,000 a year in Indianapolis as a hungry flight instructor. I started a free karate school for youth in the inner city of Indy when I started paying my dues in financial services. Since returning to my hometown of Charleston in 1999, I have been involved in Rotary Reader, organizing dozens of readers and first-grade students; a charity youth soccer tournament; Junior Achievement; and Metanoia Freedom School, which I've served for over a decade as a volunteer karate instructor in their summer enrichment program for youth. One of my proudest achievements may be helping Charleston Jazz establish a music academy while I was chairman from 2017 to 2019; now hundreds of kids have received scholarships. While much of this didn't require a penny, I could not have helped make the Jazz Academy happen if I hadn't been successful myself and utilized some of the techniques in the book, like gifts of appreciated stock or donor-advised funds. And the gratitude has always been returned. My Little Brother gave me the best hug ever after I vouched for him during a rough time in his life. Kids who thought they could beat up a black belt ended up being good students and staying off the streets. And kids who might otherwise have been written off I've seen get into good colleges and make names for themselves. Gratitude is a wonderfully vicious circle.

As we come to the end of our journey together, it's important to remember that none of these meaningful lifestyles happened by accident. They are all the result of an intentional and holistic planning process that was driven by the business owner's intense focus on their true north. If you're early in your journey, let me leave you with these nine tips to shape a more efficient and effective path to true success as you define it:

1. **Write down your life's purpose**—your mission statement—and let it be your compass through your personal and professional life, no matter what challenges the journey throws at you. Begin this process as early as possible and start planning with your true north in mind.

2. **Keep your personal and business goals aligned** as much as possible. This will smooth out your journey.

3. **Put together the best team**—with the right attitude and skills—to help you navigate safely to your destination. Great things are rarely achieved alone. The members of this team should share your values and vision, demonstrate professional excellence, and be able to advise you expertly in their specific areas. At a minimum, you'll need an attorney, an accountant, a financial adviser, a banker, an insurance professional, and a business broker. It's also recommended to pull in an industry consultant and establish a group of trustworthy peers whom you can call on for advice.

4. **Begin with a business owner's financial plan**. There is a list of personal and business documents that must be handy as you build your business and get ready for an exit. Prepare them and keep them organized so you are ready when opportunities present themselves.

5. **Know what kind of business you're running** and what that means as you grow the business and consider your exit choices. The worst thing that can happen is to be surprised near the end of your journey and find out that your business has not been built to support the type of exit you were planning. That can be catastrophic. There are pros and cons to every business model. Understanding what exits look like for your business's model will make it much easier to home in on the best financial and legal instruments to help you achieve your goals. You will also need to understand what phase your company is in. Not all companies are ready for a successful exit. Learn what needs to be done to prepare for the next phase in your business's growth.

6. **Be prepared for things to go wrong** because they will. Every business experiences challenges at some point in its growth, so plan for it. There's so much you can do to protect yourself and your business if you research the options with professionals.

7. **Make sure to enjoy the journey.** All too many business owners burn out or live their lives stressed out and frazzled. Planning and preparing can help you relax. Take care of those people and causes that are important to you.

8. **Make sure your business can run smoothly without you** well before you start trying to exit. All too often, business owners are still the backbone of their company. This is *not* attractive to investors or potential buyers. Choose an exit that fits both your financial and non-financial goals and is consistent with your compass.

9. **Grease the landing and enjoy your destination!**

Final Thoughts

Building a business is one of the most challenging and rewarding things you will ever do as a professional. For those BHBOs willing to put in the hard work and do the necessary research and planning, the return on your investment of time and money can be profound—and the good you do along the way can have an equally powerful impact on the world. I hope the guidance I have packed into *The Bottom Line of Happiness* gives you the comprehensive and specific steps you need to build an effective roadmap, as guided by your true north, and properly equip yourself for the journey. The joy that you will experience as a result of having built a successful business and funded your life's true purpose is the definition of true wealth. To quote American philosopher and psychologist William James: "The greatest use of life is to spend it for something that will outlast it."

To join the conversation and
explore more resources, visit my website:

bigheartedbusinessowner.com

Acknowledgements

I'm a numbers guy, not a writer, so I'm pretty sure my English teachers would have been horrified if they knew I had written a book. Thus, there is a long list of people who have either helped me or put up with me as I have spent the last few years writing and rewriting. First of those, is my beautiful and brilliant wife Alissa. She tolerated my absence as I spent many hours locked away writing. Hopefully, we can now return to making funny music videos again. Next, is my talented teenage son Matthew, who jokingly told me I should write "this book sucks" throughout the pages to see if anyone was actually reading it. I thought about having a prize for sending me the correct number of times the phrase was mentioned, but thought it wasn't a great idea to have readers search for "suck" within the text of a financial book. Next, is my amazing family—mom, dad, Renee, and Ben—who have believed in me throughout my life even if some of my ideas were a little hairbrained. Next, I'd like to thank those who convinced me to write a book in the first place: my former Vistage group with Kirk McMillan at the helm, Andy, Melonie, Shawn, Kerri, and Kristian. There is also a long list of friends, clients, and peers who reviewed snippets of this book to help me answer specific questions and make sure my message wasn't getting lost. At the top of this list are Ivan, Carrie, John, Pete, and Bill. I also have tremendous gratitude for Kathy Meis of Bublish and her team of editors, project managers, and designers. Finally, I need to thank my office colleagues Chris Corley and Ansley Mellette, who have both have helped me through the many challenges of writing this book. They encouraged me to finish this marathon and turn my book into something to truly help big-hearted business owners.

CPSIA information can be obtained
at www.ICGtesting.com
Printed in the USA
BVHW050031140522
636920BV00006B/11